STIR

ALSO BY CHRISTINE MANFIELD
PARAMOUNT COOKING
PARAMOUNT DESSERTS
SPICE

STIR
CHRISTINE
MANFIELD

PHOTOGRAPHY BY ASHLEY BARBER

VIKING

Viking
Penguin Books Australia Ltd
487 Maroondah Highway, PO Box 257
Ringwood, Victoria 3134, Australia
Penguin Books Ltd
Harmondsworth, Middlesex, England
Penguin Putnam Inc.
375 Hudson Street, New York, New York 10014, USA
Penguin Books Canada Limited
10 Alcorn Avenue, Toronto, Ontario, Canada M4V 3B2
Penguin Books (N.Z.) Ltd
Cnr Rosedale and Airborne Roads, Albany, Auckland, New Zealand
Penguin Books (South Africa) (Pty) Ltd
5 Watkins Street, Denver Ext 4, 2094, South Africa
Penguin Books India (P) Ltd
11, Community Centre, Panchsheel Park, New Delhi 110 017, India

First published by Penguin Books Australia Ltd 2001

10 9 8 7 6 5 4 3 2 1

Designed by Guy Mirabella
Photography by Ashley Barber
Typeset in 12/20 pt Granjon by Post Pre-press, Brisbane, Qld
Printed in China by Midas Printing (Asia) Ltd

National Library of Australia
Cataloguing-in-Publication data:

Manfield, Christine.
   Stir.

   Includes index.
   ISBN 0 670 89638 1.

   1. Cookery (Spices). I. Barber, Ashley. II. Title.

641.3383

www.penguin.com.au

STIR the pot **STIR** the senses **STIR** yourself **STIR** it up

STIR your imagination **STIR** into action **STIR** your memory

STIR fry **STIR** the blood **STIR** it round **STIR** your tastebuds

good food is essential to wellbeing **KEEP STIRRING**

Contents

Introduction

Spice pastes – hot and pungent or mellow or fragrant – are the cornerstones of many of the cuisines of the world, and certainly of the food I like to prepare and eat. Dishes made using spice pastes benefit from the preservative, digestive and antiseptic properties of spices, meaning that they are not only delicious but healthy, too. However, making your own spice pastes for use in a recipe can be complicated and time-consuming. Realising that using ready-made spice pastes would save people valuable time and, for many, remove the fear of the unknown and the intimidation of a lengthy cooking process, I embarked on the production of a commercial range of spice preparations.

After we closed the Paramount Store in 1995, we found it impossible to keep up with the demand for our products, particularly the very popular spice pastes. We were making them in the kitchen in our spare hours outside full restaurant service, and soon realised that the next big step had to be taken – getting a quality manufacturer to reproduce them, on a much larger scale, in the same way that I would make them, keeping true to their flavour without the use of preservatives or additives. And so in 2000 the Christine Manfield Spice Collection was born. I designed the products to open the door to the seductive world of spice, create harmony and equilibrium in your diet, fire your imagination and instil passion and pride in your cooking. This book is designed as a companion and guide to the range. You can either make the spice pastes from scratch following the basic recipes at the start of each chapter, or purchase them ready-made when you find yourself short of time. Using the ready-made products is a totally acceptable short cut!

The recipes in the book build on my comprehensive volume *Spice* and celebrate the diversity of contemporary everyday Australian cooking. Each recipe given here will provide maximum flavour and seasoning for your food. The preparations include fast, hot cooking such as stir-frying or barbecuing, and long, slow methods, such as braising, that don't require constant attention – you can leave the dish to work miracles unchecked while you busy yourself elsewhere. The recipes showcase the versatility of each product and have been devised with the intention of using minimum effort for maximum effect and taste. Rather than complex, restaurant-style cooking that necessitates several preparations and steps to reach the final outcome, these recipes are designed for simple cooking at home. I hope they will inspire you to get busy in your kitchen.

I remain a staunch advocate of the philosophy that life is too short to eat bad food. Please join me in that quest by taking an active interest in good, healthy, interesting cooking with spice pastes.

NOTE   If you are using the ready-made products from my range, each jar contains roughly 12 portions for any given preparation.

Chilli Jam

My chilli jam is more complex and refined than many of its commercial counterparts (sambals, etc.) and you'll find it has a multitude of uses in many of the recipes in this book beyond this chapter. I'm sure you'll find it useful in some of your favourite recipes, too. Slow, prolonged cooking time gives it an enduring and lingering sweetness, but although it is referred to as a jam, it is not to be confused with confectionery jams or jellies – spread it on toast for breakfast at your peril! The basic recipe on page 6 does not translate easily into a smaller quantity, but don't worry – it quickly disappears because it's so addictive.

1.5 kg/3 lb large red Chinese chillies, chopped
300 g/9½ oz red birds-eye chillies, chopped
8 large brown onions, chopped
15 large cloves garlic, chopped
1 litre/32 fl oz vegetable oil
300 ml/10 fl oz Tamarind Liquid (page 200)
125 g/4 oz palm sugar/jaggery, shaved
extra vegetable oil, for sealing

Chilli jam

1 Blend chilli, onion, garlic and oil to a smooth paste in a food processor. **2** Cook paste in a wide, heavy-based pan over low heat until dark red – this will take up to 12 hours of continuous slow cooking and occasional stirring. **3** Stir in tamarind liquid and palm sugar and cook very slowly for 2 hours more. **4** Spoon into sterilised jars, cover with a film of oil and seal when cool. Keeps, refrigerated, for up to 3 months.

Makes 2 litres/64 fl oz

2 medium-size brown onions, finely chopped
3 large cloves garlic, finely chopped
1 tablespoon finely chopped ginger
4 red birds-eye chillies, finely chopped
20 ml/¾ fl oz vegetable oil
250 g/8 oz crunchy peanut butter
12 teaspoons CHILLI JAM (page 6)
400 ml/12½ fl oz coconut milk
125 ml/4 fl oz light soy sauce
150 g/5 oz brown sugar
80 ml/2½ fl oz strained lime juice
100 ml/3 fl oz rice vinegar
50 ml/1½ fl oz fish sauce

Peanut chilli sauce

1 Sweat onion, garlic, ginger and chilli in oil over moderate heat until softened. **2** Add peanut butter, CHILLI JAM and coconut milk and bring to the boil, stirring frequently to prevent sticking. Cook, uncovered, over gentle heat for 15 minutes, or until thickened. **3** Add remaining ingredients, bring back to the boil and cook for 5 minutes. **4** Taste and, if necessary, adjust seasoning. Serve with satay prawns or chicken, grilled meats or gado-gado (vegetable) salad. Will keep, refrigerated in a sealed container, for up to 2 weeks. Reheat gently to serve.

Makes 1 litre/32 fl oz

Chilli salt beancurd with bean sprout salad

4 stems Chinese broccoli/gai lan, sliced
200 g/6½ oz bean sprouts
12 snow peas, finely sliced
250 g/8 oz snow pea sprouts
50 g/1½ oz tatsoi leaves *or* watercress sprigs
vegetable oil, for deep-frying
8 fresh beancurd/tofu squares
4 teaspoons CHILLI JAM (page 6)
1 large red Chinese *or* Dutch chilli, seeded and
    cut into julienne
6 green onions/scallions, sliced diagonally
Chilli salt crust
2 large dried Chinese *or* Dutch chillies
4 black peppercorns
1 teaspoon sea salt
2 tablespoons rice flour
Chilli dressing
60 ml/2 fl oz fish sauce
1 clove garlic, finely chopped
1 red birds-eye chilli, finely chopped
3 teaspoons strained lime juice
2 teaspoons caster sugar

1 To make the chilli salt crust, dry-roast chillies, peppercorns and sea salt over gentle heat until slightly coloured. Cool, then grind to a fine powder and mix with rice flour. **2** To make the salad, steam broccoli for a few minutes until tender (the stems will take longer than the leaves, so remove the leaves as they cook or add halfway through to ensure even cooking). Combine broccoli with bean sprouts, snow peas, snow pea sprouts and tatsoi. **3** Mix chilli dressing ingredients thoroughly and pour over salad. Toss well and allow to stand for 15 minutes before serving. **4** To cook beancurd, heat oil in a deep-fryer or large pot to 180°C/350°F. Coat beancurd squares with chilli salt crust and fry, a few at a time, for 2 minutes, or until pale golden and crisp on the surface. They will float to the top when cooked. Remove carefully with a mesh spoon and drain on paper towel. **5** Arrange salad on plates, sit the fried beancurd on top with the CHILLI JAM, chilli strips and green onion and serve.

Serves 4

Crispy sweet-and-sour fish with cucumber salad

vegetable oil, for deep-frying
2 teaspoons Sichuan Spice Salt (page 200)
1 tablespoon rice flour
8 whole small garfish *or* whiting, cleaned and scaled

Chilli sauce
20 ml/¾ fl oz vegetable oil
4 green onions/scallions, finely sliced
2 cloves garlic, finely chopped
1 teaspoon finely chopped ginger
4 teaspoons CHILLI JAM (page 6)
40 ml/1¼ fl oz Chinese black vinegar
20 ml/¾ fl oz light soy sauce
2 teaspoons fish sauce
2 tablespoons caster sugar
100 ml/3 fl oz White Chicken Stock (page 202)

Cucumber salad
1 cucumber, peeled and seeded
4 green onions/scallions, finely sliced
1 large red Chinese *or* Dutch chilli, finely sliced
2 tablespoons peanuts, roasted and chopped
¼ cup shredded mint leaves

1 To make chilli sauce, heat oil in a wok and fry green onion, garlic and ginger for 30 seconds, or until fragrant. Add CHILLI JAM, vinegar, soy sauce, fish sauce and sugar and simmer for 3 minutes. Add stock and simmer for another 5 minutes. Set aside and reheat when ready to serve. **2** To make cucumber salad, cut cucumber into small pieces and mix in a bowl with green onion, chilli, peanuts and mint. **3** To cook fish, heat oil in a deep-fryer or large pot to 180°C/350°F. Mix spice salt with flour and coat each fish with seasoned flour. Deep-fry fish for 4–6 minutes, depending on size and thickness. Remove from oil carefully and drain on paper towel. **4** To serve, divide cucumber salad between 4 plates, sit crispy fish on top and spoon chilli sauce over.

Serves 4

200 g/6½ oz jasmine rice, washed
cold water
2 teaspoons sea salt, roasted and ground
2 red birds-eye chillies, roasted and ground
2 tablespoons rice flour
4 × 125 g/4 oz snapper fillets (see Note)
100 ml/3 fl oz olive oil
½ cup coriander/cilantro/Chinese parsley leaves
8 teaspoons CHILLI JAM (page 6)
1 tablespoon Fried Garlic Slices (page 201)

Pan-fried snapper fillets with steamed rice and chilli jam

1 Put rice in a saucepan and add enough cold water to measure 4 cm/1½ in over rice. Cover with a lid and cook on moderate heat for about 15 minutes, or until water has been absorbed and rice is soft and fluffy. **2** Mix salt, chilli and rice flour together. Coat snapper fillets with seasoned flour. **3** Heat oil in a frying pan until hot and shallow-fry fish over moderate heat until cooked, turning halfway through. Cooking time should be about 6 minutes (3 minutes on each side). Flesh should be white and firm without being dry or breaking open. **4** Remove fish from pan and rest on paper towel. **5** Spoon hot rice onto plates, sit fish on top and garnish with coriander leaves, CHILLI JAM and fried garlic slices.

Serves 4

Note: Other suitable fish include mackerel, cod, sea bass, gurnard, bream, sea mullet or any tropical reef fish.

8 large (1 week old) eggs
1 teaspoon sea salt
40 ml/1¼ fl oz light soy sauce
20 ml/¾ fl oz dark soy sauce
3 star anise
2 tablespoons Chinese oolong/black tea leaves
1 tablespoon jasmine tea leaves
8 teaspoons CHILLI JAM (page 6)
selection of condiments, to serve (optional)

Spiced tea eggs with chilli jam

1 Cook eggs in simmering water for 8 minutes, or until hard-boiled. Remove from heat and plunge into cold water. Crack shells gently with a spoon until finely cracked all over. Put eggs in a saucepan with remaining ingredients, except CHILLI JAM and condiments. **2** Cover with water and bring to the boil. Cover pot, reduce heat to low and simmer for 30 minutes. Remove pot from heat and allow eggs to cool in tea infusion for 3–4 hours for flavour to develop fully. **3** Remove eggs from liquid and carefully peel off cracked shells. The eggs should have a marbled appearance. **4** Cut eggs in half and serve with CHILLI JAM as a condiment along with pickled vegetables/jiang cai, preserved mustard greens/gai choy, or Chinese cabbage/bai choy. These preserves are readily available from Chinese grocers.

Serves 4

Crab, pork and chilli dumplings

24 won ton wrappers
1 egg white
rice flour

Crab and pork stuffing

75 g/2½ oz lean minced pork
2 teaspoons Chinese Shaoxing rice wine
½ teaspoon freshly ground white pepper
200 g/6½ oz cooked crabmeat
2 Chinese cabbage/bai choy leaves, blanched
   and shredded
8 water chestnuts, finely diced
4 stalks Chinese celery/kun choy *or* plain celery,
   finely chopped
2 green onions/scallions, finely sliced
2 tablespoons chopped coriander/cilantro/
   Chinese parsley leaves
2 teaspoons finely chopped ginger
2 teaspoons fish sauce
2 teaspoons light soy sauce
2 teaspoons CHILLI JAM (page 6)

Dipping sauce

50 ml/1½ fl oz Chinese black vinegar
1 teaspoon finely shredded ginger

1 To make stuffing, knead pork mince with rice wine and white pepper in a bowl. Add remaining ingredients, mixing thoroughly by hand to combine. Roll into 24 small balls and flatten slightly with your fingers. **2** Lay out 4 won ton wrappers at a time on the bench. Place stuffing on centre of each wrapper, brush edges lightly with egg white and fold over, pressing edges together to seal. Wrap around finger and press ends together. **3** Lay prepared dumplings in a single layer on a tray sprinkled with rice flour to prevent sticking. Continue to make dumplings until stuffing mix is all used. **4** Cook dumplings, several at a time, in boiling water for 3 minutes. Remove carefully with a slotted spoon. **5** Make dipping sauce by combining black vinegar and ginger shreds. Serve dumplings with sauce.

Serves 4

4 large eggs

40 ml/1¼ fl oz vegetable oil

4 teaspoons CHILLI JAM (page 6)

2 teaspoons BLACK PEPPER AND LEMONGRASS STIR-FRY
    PASTE (page 82)

2 teaspoons chilli bean paste/toban jiang

200 ml/6½ fl oz Prawn/Shrimp Stock (page 202) *or* White
    Chicken Stock (page 202)

410 g/13 oz fresh Hokkien egg noodles

125 g/4 oz cha siew/Chinese red roasted pork, sliced

12 green king prawns/shrimp, shelled and deveined

2 squid tubes, cleaned and cut lengthwise into thin strips

200 g/6½ oz bean sprouts

2 large red Chinese *or* Dutch chillies, finely sliced

4 tablespoons coriander/cilantro/Chinese parsley leaves

Combination stir-fried Hokkien egg noodles

1 Beat 3 of the eggs in a bowl. Heat half the oil in a wok and add beaten egg, tilting pan to make a thin omelette. Cook until set. Turn out of wok, roll up and slice finely. Set aside. **2** Heat remaining oil in wok and fry CHILLI JAM, BLACK PEPPER AND LEMONGRASS STIR-FRY PASTE and chilli bean paste together for 1 minute, or until fragrant. **3** Mix in stock and, when simmering, add noodles and toss to combine. Cook for 3 minutes, or until noodles have softened. Add remaining egg, stirring quickly with a chopstick so egg forms threads through the sauce. **4** Add pork, prawns and squid and continue to toss over high heat until just cooked, about 2 minutes. Add bean sprouts and omelette strips. **5** Sprinkle with chilli slices and coriander leaves and serve.

Serves 4

Chicken and stir-fried chilli vegetables

4 chicken thighs
40 ml/1¼ fl oz light soy sauce
2 teaspoons sesame oil
vegetable oil, for deep-frying
1 teaspoon Sichuan Spice Salt (page 200)
1 tablespoon finely chopped garlic
2 teaspoons finely chopped ginger
2 red birds-eye chillies, finely chopped
1 teaspoon freshly ground black pepper
40 ml/1¼ fl oz fish sauce
20 ml/¾ fl oz Chinese oyster sauce
6 Chinese white cabbage/bok choy hearts, blanched
   and halved lengthwise
12 snow peas, trimmed
200 g/6½ oz bean sprouts
½ red capsicum/bell pepper, finely sliced
8 teaspoons CHILLI JAM (page 6)
1 cup Thai/holy basil leaves

1 Cut each chicken thigh into 2 pieces at the joint. Mix soy sauce with sesame oil and rub into flesh of chicken. **2** Heat vegetable oil in a deep-fryer or large pot to 180°C/350°F and fry chicken pieces, a few at a time, for 8 minutes, or until crisp and golden. Check flesh is cooked by inserting a skewer – flesh should be pink and juices should run clear. Remove chicken from oil with a slotted spoon and rest on paper towel. Sprinkle with Sichuan spice salt. **3** Heat a wok, add about 1 tablespoon vegetable oil and fry garlic, ginger, chilli and black pepper for a few seconds until fragrant. **4** Add fish and oyster sauces, then toss in bok choy, snow peas, bean sprouts, capsicum strips and CHILLI JAM. Cook over high heat, tossing to combine, for 1–2 minutes, or until vegetables have wilted. **5** Add basil leaves, toss and remove from heat immediately. **6** Arrange stir-fried vegetables in a pile on plates and top with fried chicken pieces. Serve extra CHILLI JAM as a condiment, if desired.

Serves 4

Eggplant sambal with chilli pork

8 Japanese/Asian eggplants/aubergines, trimmed
6 Chinese cabbage/bai choy leaves
2 teaspoons Chinese Shaoxing rice wine
2 teaspoons fish sauce
½ teaspoon freshly ground white pepper
80 g/2½ oz lean minced pork
20 ml/¾ fl oz vegetable oil
4 green onions/scallions, finely sliced
1 teaspoon finely chopped ginger
1 teaspoon finely chopped garlic
1 red birds-eye chilli, finely chopped
4 teaspoons CHILLI JAM (page 6)
20 ml/¾ fl oz light soy sauce
20 ml/¾ fl oz Chinese black vinegar
2 teaspoons caster sugar
1 teaspoon sesame oil
¼ cup coriander/cilantro/Chinese parsley leaves

1 Cut eggplants into quarters lengthwise, to make thick batons. **2** Line a large steamer basket with cabbage leaves and lay eggplant slices on the cabbage in a single layer. Cover with lid and steam over boiling water for 15 minutes, or until eggplant has wilted and is tender. Discard cabbage leaves when eggplant is cooked. Remove and discard skin from eggplant. **3** While eggplant is steaming, work rice wine, fish sauce and pepper through minced pork with your fingers, kneading thoroughly. **4** Heat oil in a wok and fry green onion, ginger, garlic and chilli for 30 seconds, or until fragrant. **5** Add CHILLI JAM, soy sauce, vinegar and sugar and, when simmering, add pork. Toss over high heat to ensure even cooking. Cook for 5 minutes, or until pork has browned. Taste and, if necessary, adjust seasoning. **6** To serve, arrange steamed eggplant slices on a large plate and spoon chilli pork over. Drizzle with sesame oil and sprinkle with coriander leaves.
Serves 4

1 × 1.5 kg/3 lb Chinese roasted duck
400 g/12½ oz fresh rice noodle sheets, cut into
   2 cm/¾ in wide strips
2 teaspoons sesame oil
20 ml/¾ fl oz vegetable oil
2 teaspoons chilli oil
2 cloves garlic, finely chopped
2 small red birds-eye chillies, finely chopped
1 teaspoon finely chopped ginger
4 teaspoons CHILLI JAM (page 6)
1 Chinese pork/lap cheong sausage, finely sliced
200 g/6½ oz bean sprouts
6 green onions/scallions, finely sliced
40 ml/1¼ fl oz sweet soy sauce/kecap manis
2 teaspoons fish sauce
2 eggs, beaten
1 bunch garlic chives, snipped
1 tablespoon Fried Garlic Slices (page 201)

Roasted duck noodles with chilli

1 Slice meat and crispy skin from duck and cut into 2.5 cm/1 in pieces. Discard bones and fat. **2** Put noodles in a pot and pour boiling water over to soften. Drain noodles in a colander and toss with sesame oil to prevent sticking. **3** Heat wok, add vegetable and chilli oils and fry garlic, chilli and ginger briefly. **4** Add CHILLI JAM, sausage slices, bean sprouts and green onion and toss over heat. Add duck pieces and cook until heated through, about 90 seconds. Tip into a bowl. **5** Return wok to heat and toss rice noodles with sweet soy and fish sauces over high heat for 2 minutes. **6** Put noodles into the bowl with already-cooked ingredients and add beaten egg to the wok. As it starts to set, throw the noodles and duck back into the wok and toss so that noodles are coated with egg. **7** Pile noodles onto plates, sprinkle with garlic chives and fried garlic slices and serve.

Serves 4

1 × 1 kg/2 lb piece of belly pork, with skin
4 teaspoons sea salt
4 teaspoons Chinese Five-spice Powder (page 200)
1 teaspoon Sichuan peppercorns, roasted and ground
1 teaspoon sesame oil
1 bunch Chinese broccoli/gai lan, washed
40 ml/1¼ fl oz Chinese oyster sauce
4 teaspoons CHILLI JAM (page 6)

Five-spice roasted belly pork

1 Bring a large pot of water to boiling point. Add belly pork and blanch for 3 minutes. Remove from pot and set aside to cool for 10 minutes. **2** Mix salt with five-spice powder and ground pepper. Rub pork with sesame oil, then rub spiced salt liberally into pork, covering all surfaces. Stand at room temperature for 2 hours. **3** Preheat oven to hot (220°C/450°F). Lay belly pork on a wire rack over a roasting tray that is one-third full of hot water. Place in centre of oven and roast for 40 minutes. Reduce heat slightly to 200°C/400°F, toss out water from roasting tray and continue to dry-roast pork for another 20 minutes, or until it is tender and the skin is crisp. Test with a skewer and, if juices run clear, meat is cooked. Remove pork from the oven and let rest in a warm place for 15 minutes before slicing. **4** Cut broccoli into 5 cm/2 in lengths, including stems and leaves, peeling any thick stems if necessary. Cook in boiling water for a few minutes until softened. Remove from water and toss with oyster sauce in a pan over high heat until evenly coated. **5** Lay cooked broccoli on serving plates. Cut pork into thick slices, arrange over broccoli and serve with CHILLI JAM. Sichuan Spice Salt (page 200) and lemon wedges could be served as additional condiments.

Serves 4

8 dried Chinese black mushrooms
1 × 1 kg/2 lb piece of belly pork, with skin
2 litres/64 fl oz Red Braising Stock (page 203)
vegetable oil, for deep-frying
steamed rice, to serve
4 teaspoons CHILLI JAM (page 6)
1 bunch garlic chives, cut into 1 cm/½ in lengths

Red-cooked pork with chilli jam

1 Soak dried mushrooms in boiling water to cover for 30 minutes. Remove from water and cut off stems. Discard water. **2** Meanwhile, cut belly pork into 4 even pieces. Put in a large pot, cover with cold water and bring to the boil. Simmer for 5 minutes, remove from heat and drain meat in colander. Rinse thoroughly under cold water. **3** Bring stock to boiling point in a large pot. Add pork, reduce heat and simmer very gently, stirring occasionally, for 30 minutes. **4** Turn off heat, add softened mushrooms and leave with pork in stock for a further 20 minutes, or until meat is tender and glossy in appearance. Remove pork and mushrooms from pot with a slotted spoon. Drain on paper towel. **5** Heat oil in a deep-fryer or large pot to 180°C/350°F and fry pork for 5 minutes, or until outer surfaces are crisp and caramelised in appearance. **6** Slice each piece of pork in half and serve with steamed rice, CHILLI JAM and a sprinkling of garlic chives. Add a spoonful of the pot juices and some steamed green vegetables, if desired.

Serves 4

10 red shallots, chopped
10 cloves garlic, chopped
2 stalks lemongrass, chopped
4 slices fresh galangal, chopped
40 ml/1¼ fl oz vegetable oil
2 teaspoons ground turmeric
8 teaspoons CHILLI JAM (page 6)
2 kg/4½ lbs oxtail, cut into 4 cm/1¼ in pieces
6 ripe tomatoes, quartered
400 ml/12½ fl oz tomato purée
2 litres/64 fl oz White Chicken Stock (page 202) *or* water
500 ml/16 fl oz Tamarind Liquid (page 200)
60 g/2 oz palm sugar/jaggery, shaved
4 large red Chinese *or* Dutch chillies, split lengthwise
3 kaffir lime leaves
fish sauce
freshly ground black pepper
4 tablespoons Fried Shallot Slices (page 201)
steamed white rice *or* fresh rice noodles, to serve

Hot-and-sour braised oxtail

1 Using a food processor or mortar and pestle, blend shallots, garlic, lemongrass and galangal to a paste with oil, turmeric and CHILLI JAM. Put into a large dish with oxtail pieces, tomato and tomato purée and marinate for 2 hours or overnight. **2** In a large pot, bring stock to simmering point with tamarind liquid and palm sugar. Add oxtail and its marinade, chilli and lime leaves. Simmer over low heat, uncovered, for at least 2½ hours or until oxtail is tender and liquid has reduced by about half. The slower the cooking, the better the result. **3** Season to taste with fish sauce and pepper, adding enough of each to balance the flavours. Sprinkle with fried shallot slices and serve with rice or noodles.

Serves 4

Note: This dish will develop even more flavour if prepared a day in advance to the point of adding the fish sauce and pepper. Add seasonings and gently reheat over low heat the next day.

Harissa

Harissa is a staple in the North African, and more specifically the Tunisian, diet. It is used to add both flavour and colour to many preparations. Harissa is a counterpart to an Asian sambal, although very much hotter on the palate as it has not been mellowed by cooking or had the addition of sugar. It has a fiery taste and is traditionally served as a condiment, like a relish. It is great with oil and a little lemon juice for dipping bread, for mixing with olives, to enhance salads or soups and cooked fish and meats, as well as being an automatic addition to any cous cous preparation. As with all chilli preparations, test the water first – taste – and then use harissa accordingly. The heat of the relish can be varied according to the type of dried chillies used in the preparation. I use the larger dried Chinese or New Mexican chillies, but if you want to give it an extra kick, add a few dried birds-eye or other small Asian chillies, or the fiery habaneros.

75 g/2½ oz large dried Chinese *or* Dutch chillies,
  chopped
2 teaspoons cumin seeds
¼ teaspoon caraway seeds
2 large cloves garlic, chopped
1 teaspoon sea salt
50 ml/1½ fl oz tomato purée
60 ml/2 fl oz olive oil

Harissa

1 Soak chilli in a little water for 2 hours. Drain, reserving soaking water. **2** Dry-roast cumin seeds over gentle heat until fragrant. Cool, then grind to a fine powder with caraway seeds. **3** Blend chilli, garlic and 100 ml/3½ fl oz reserved soaking water in a food processor, then add spices, salt and tomato purée. With motor running, slowly pour in oil and blend until paste is smooth. **4** Spoon into a sterilised jar, cover with a film of oil and seal. Keeps, refrigerated, for up to 1 month.

Makes about 250 ml/8 fl oz

1 bulb/head garlic

extra-virgin olive oil

4 tomatoes

sea salt

freshly ground black pepper

1.2 litres/38 fl oz White Chicken Stock (page 202)

400 g/12½ oz cooked chickpeas

1 teaspoon cumin seeds, roasted and ground

4 teaspoons HARISSA (page 26)

2 tablespoons finely chopped flat-leaf parsley

1 tablespoon shredded mint leaves

1 tablespoon diced red/Spanish onion

Chickpea and harissa soup

1 Preheat oven to moderate (180°C/350°F). Cut top off garlic bulb, drizzle with a little olive oil and wrap in foil. Cut tomatoes in half lengthwise, drizzle with a little olive oil and season with salt and pepper. **2** Roast garlic and tomatoes for 30 minutes, or until garlic is soft and tomato is soft and coloured. Unwrap and squeeze roasted garlic cloves from their skins. Discard skins. **3** In a large pot, bring stock, chickpeas, garlic and tomato to boiling point. Stir in cumin, 1 teaspoon salt, ½ teaspoon pepper and HARISSA and simmer for 10 minutes. Taste and, if necessary, adjust seasoning. **4** Swirl in herbs, diced onion and 20 ml/¾ fl oz olive oil and serve soup with crusty bread. Additions can include a coddled egg, shredded chicken, or crispy bacon or pancetta strips, depending on your preference.

Serves 4

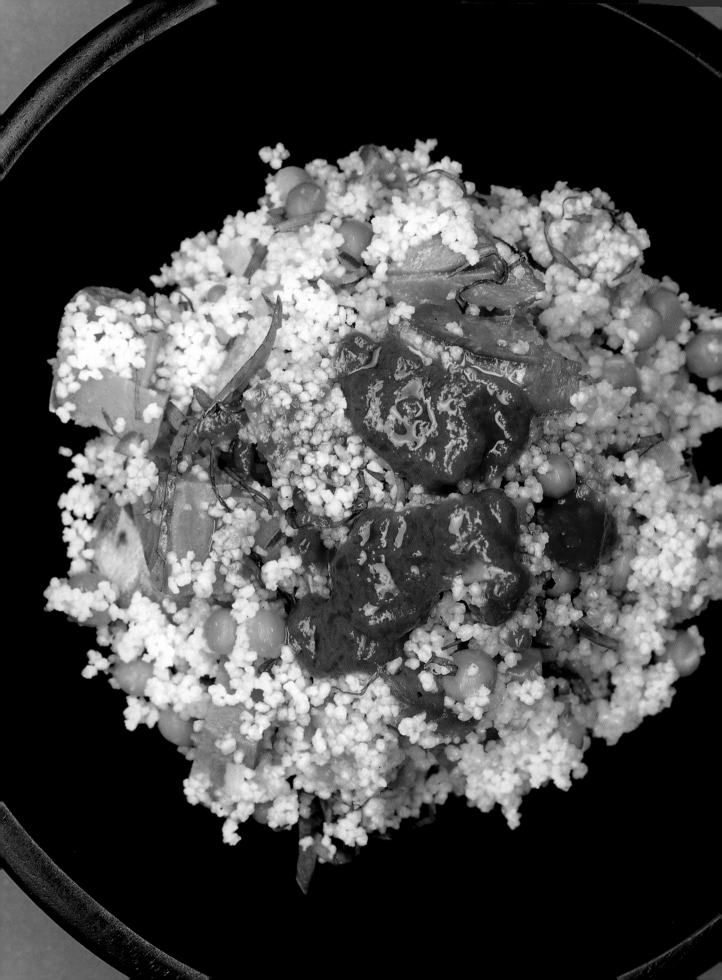

200 g/6½ oz sweet potato, cut into 2.5 cm/1 in dice
200 g/6½ oz pumpkin, cut into 2.5 cm/1 in dice
40 ml/1¼ fl oz olive oil
1 teaspoon sea salt
1 teaspoon freshly ground black pepper
300 ml/10 fl oz Spiced Vegetable Stock (page 204)
  or water
200 g/6½ oz cous cous
60 g/2 oz unsalted butter
100 g/3½ oz fresh peas, blanched
1 red/Spanish onion, finely diced
4 teaspoons diced PRESERVED LEMON (page 124)
2 tablespoons shredded mint leaves
4 teaspoons HARISSA (page 26)
Salad dressing
125 ml/4 fl oz extra-virgin olive oil
15 ml/½ fl oz red-wine vinegar
20 ml/¾ fl oz lemon juice, strained
sea salt
freshly ground black pepper

Roasted vegetable and cous cous salad

1 Preheat oven to moderately hot (200°C/400°F). **2** To make salad dressing, whisk olive oil, vinegar and lemon juice and season to taste with salt and pepper. **3** Put sweet potato and pumpkin into a roasting tray and add olive oil, salt and pepper. Bake for 25 minutes, or until golden and soft. Remove from oven and set aside. **4** Bring stock to boiling point in a saucepan and pour in cous cous, stirring continuously. Remove from heat, stir in butter, cover pan and allow to sit for about 15 minutes, or until cous cous has absorbed all the liquid. Fluff with a fork. **5** Put cous cous into a large bowl and stir through baked vegetables, peas, red onion, PRESERVED LEMON and mint. **6** Spoon salad onto plates, drizzle with dressing and add a teaspoon of HARISSA to each serving.

Serves 4

Vegetable hotpot

20 ml/¾ fl oz olive oil

1 medium-size brown onion, quartered

2 tablespoons diced red capsicum/bell pepper

2 cloves garlic, finely chopped

2 teaspoons ras el hanout spice mix

2 teaspoons HARISSA (page 26)

1.5 litres/48 fl oz Spiced Vegetable Stock (page 204)

2 potatoes, peeled and cut into eighths

1 turnip, peeled and cut into eighths

1 parsnip, peeled and cut into thick rounds

2 zucchini/courgettes, cut into 5 cm/2 in lengths

4 broccoli florets

4 tomatoes, quartered

20 ml/¾ fl oz lemon juice

2 teaspoons sea salt

1 teaspoon freshly ground black pepper

3 tablespoons coriander/cilantro/Chinese parsley leaves

2 tablespoons shredded mint leaves

cous cous *or* steamed rice, to serve

1 Heat oil in a large frying pan and fry onion, capsicum and garlic until softened. Add ras el hanout and HARISSA and fry for another 3 minutes, or until fragrant. **2** Add stock and bring to simmering point. Add potato and turnip and simmer for 15 minutes. Add remaining vegetables and simmer for another 25 minutes, or until vegetables are soft and cooked. **3** Add lemon juice and season with salt and pepper. Remove from heat and stir in herbs. **4** Serve with cous cous or rice. Extra HARISSA can be served as a condiment, if desired.

Serves 4

2 cooked chicken breasts

300 g/9½ oz short pasta (penne, rigatoni *or* spirals)

sea salt

80 ml/2½ fl oz extra-virgin olive oil

1 medium-size onion, finely sliced

4 cloves garlic, finely chopped

2 small red birds-eye *or* serrano chillies, seeded and
   finely chopped

2 teaspoons HARISSA (page 26)

¾ cup roasted-tomato pasta sauce (any commercially
   available brand)

½ teaspoon freshly ground black pepper

½ cup finely chopped flat-leaf parsley

100 g/3½ oz fetta cheese, diced (see Note)

Pasta with chicken, fetta and harissa

1 Shred chicken and set aside. **2** Bring a pot of water to the boil, add pasta and 1 teaspoon sea salt and cook until pasta is al dente. Strain. **3** While pasta is cooking, heat olive oil in a frying pan and fry onion until it starts to colour. Add garlic and chilli and cook for 1 minute, or until fragrant. **4** Add HARISSA and tomato pasta sauce and cook for 5 minutes on moderate heat. Season with salt and pepper. Stir in chicken and simmer for about 2 minutes, or until meat has heated through. Remove from heat. **5** Toss chicken mixture, parsley and fetta through pasta and serve immediately.

Serves 4

Note: Ricotta can be substituted for fetta.

Spiced ratatouille

1 × 300 g/9½ oz eggplant/aubergine, cut into
   2 cm/¾ in cubes
sea salt
100 ml/3½ fl oz olive oil
1 medium-size onion, diced
3 cloves garlic, finely chopped
½ teaspoon ground coriander
½ teaspoon ground cumin
2 red capsicums/bell peppers, seeded and cut into
   2 cm/¾ in pieces
4 small zucchini/courgettes, diced
4 tomatoes, peeled and diced
2 teaspoons HARISSA (page 26)
¼ cup finely chopped flat-leaf parsley
freshly ground black pepper

1 Lay eggplant on a tray in a single layer and salt lightly. Leave for 30 minutes, then rub off salt and excess liquid with a paper towel. 2 Heat oil in a large lidded frying pan and gently fry onion, garlic and spices until fragrant. 3 Add eggplant and capsicum, cover with lid and cook over low heat for 25 minutes, or until very soft. 4 Add zucchini and tomato and cook, covered, for a further 15 minutes. 5 Stir in HARISSA and parsley and season to taste with salt and pepper. Serve hot, warm or at room temperature with grilled meats or fish, or as a starter with crusty bread.

Serves 4

Duck and lemon risotto with harissa

1 × 2 kg/4½ lb duck, roasted *or* braised
1.2 litres/38 fl oz White Chicken Stock (page 202)
1 tablespoon unsalted butter
40 ml/1¼ fl oz fruity extra-virgin olive oil
1 large brown onion, diced
4 cloves garlic, minced
1 fennel bulb, diced
rind/zest of 2 lemons, blanched and minced
400 g/12½ oz arborio rice
125 ml/4 fl oz white wine
20 ml/¾ fl oz lemon juice
1 teaspoon sea salt
½ teaspoon freshly ground black pepper
½ cup lemon basil *or* basil leaves, torn
4 teaspoons HARISSA (page 26)

1 Using your fingers, shred meat from duck and set aside. Discard skin, fat and bones. 2 Bring stock to boiling point, then reduce heat to a low simmer. 3 Heat butter and oil in a wide-based pan and fry onion, garlic and fennel until softened and beginning to colour. Add lemon rind. Stir in rice and fry gently until it is well coated with the aromatics. Add wine and cook over medium heat until wine has been absorbed. Stirring continuously, gradually add hot stock, a ladleful at a time, adding each new ladleful when the last one has been absorbed. By the last ladleful, the rice should be nearly cooked – this will take about 20 minutes. 4 With the last application of stock, stir through shredded duck meat and lemon juice. Season and cook for 2–3 minutes. Remove from heat and stir lemon basil leaves through. Serve immediately with HARISSA as a condiment.

Serves 4

20 ml/¾ fl oz olive oil

8 lamb shanks

8 spring onions, white bulbs only, peeled

8 cloves garlic

2 small red birds-eye *or* serrano chillies, sliced

200 ml/6½ fl oz red wine

1.2 litres/38 fl oz Beef/Veal Stock (page 203)
  or Brown Chicken Stock (page 202)

2 sprigs of rosemary

1 bay leaf

800 ml/26 fl oz water

170 g/5½ oz polenta/cornmeal

50 g/1½ oz unsalted butter

1 teaspoon sea salt

1 teaspoon freshly ground black pepper

1 teaspoon ground chilli *or* paprika

8 teaspoons HARISSA (page 26)

Slow-cooked lamb shanks with polenta and harissa

1 Preheat oven to moderately low (160°C/325°F). Heat oil in a large heavy-based, flameproof roasting tray and fry shanks on all sides for about 10 minutes, or until brown. Remove from tray and set aside. **2** In the same roasting tray, fry spring onion bulbs, garlic and chilli for a few minutes. Add wine and bring to the boil. Cook for 5 minutes, then add stock, rosemary and bay leaf. **3** Bring to the boil, reduce heat to a simmer and return shanks to tray. Cover and cook in oven for 2 hours. **4** While shanks are cooking, prepare polenta. Bring water to the boil in a large saucepan and pour in polenta. Reduce heat to low and whisk to combine. Cook polenta over heat, stirring, for 25–30 minutes, or until cooked. (It is cooked when it comes away cleanly from sides of pan and appears homogenous.) If it gets too dry and stiff during cooking, add a little more water. Stir in butter and season with salt, pepper and ground chilli. Remove from heat. **5** Remove shanks, onions and garlic from tray with a slotted spoon and keep warm. **6** Pour stock into a saucepan and boil over high heat until reduced by half. Strain through a fine mesh sieve. Stir half the HARISSA into the smooth sauce. **7** Spoon soft polenta onto plates and sit lamb shanks, onions and garlic on top. Ladle some sauce over and add a teaspoon of the remaining HARISSA to each serving.

Serves 4

8 lemon slices

4 sprigs of dill

4 whole, plate-size fish (snapper, rouget, whiting etc.),
   cleaned, scaled and rinsed

1 teaspoon sea salt

1 teaspoon freshly ground black pepper

40 ml/1¼ fl oz extra-virgin olive oil

2 teaspoons HARISSA (page 26)

2 teaspoons lemon juice

vegetable oil, for deep-frying basil leaves

½ cup basil leaves

Grilled fish with harissa dressing

1 Put 2 lemon slices and 1 sprig of dill in cavity of each fish. Season fish liberally with salt and pepper. Drizzle 30 ml olive oil over fish to prevent sticking during cooking and place fish on a baking tray. 2 Mix HARISSA with the remaining olive oil and the lemon juice. 3 Heat some vegetable oil in a deep-fryer or saucepan to 180°C/350°F and deep-fry basil leaves for about 20 seconds, or until crisp. Drain on paper towel. 4 Cook fish under a griller for 6 minutes, then flip over and cook for another 3–5 minutes, depending on thickness. Flesh should be white and firm without being dry or breaking open. 5 Remove lemon and dill from cavity and spoon HARISSA dressing over fish. Sprinkle with deep-fried basil leaves to serve.

Serves 4

Spicy sausages with onion, tomato and harissa

olive oil

4 medium-size brown onions, sliced

6 cloves garlic, finely sliced

1 teaspoon cumin seeds, roasted and ground

6 ripe tomatoes, peeled and quartered *or*
  1 × 400 g/12½ oz can tomatoes, drained

2 tablespoons chopped oregano

1 teaspoon sea salt

1 teaspoon freshly ground black pepper

8 spicy lamb Merguez *or* other sausages

4 teaspoons HARISSA (page 26)

1 Preheat oven to hot (220°C/450°F). **2** Heat oil in a frying pan and fry onion, garlic and cumin over moderate heat for 10 minutes, or until starting to colour. Stir in tomato and cook, covered, for another 15 minutes, or until tomato starts to lose its form. Stir in oregano and season with salt and pepper. **3** Grill sausages for about 10 minutes, or until brown on all sides. Transfer to oven to cook for a further 5–6 minutes. **4** Serve sausages with tomato mixture, HARISSA and crusty bread.

Serves 4

40 ml/1¼ fl oz olive oil

8 teaspoons HARISSA (page 26)

1 × 600 g/1 lb 3 oz beef tenderloin *or* Scotch fillet

extra HARISSA, to serve

Bean salad

125 ml/4 fl oz extra-virgin olive oil

1 small onion, diced

2 cloves garlic, finely chopped

1 small red birds-eye *or* serrano chilli, seeded and
   finely chopped

2 teaspoons ground cumin

100 g/3½ oz green Puy lentils, washed

200 ml/6½ fl oz White Chicken Stock (page 202)
   or water

100 g/3½ oz green beans, sliced

100 g/3½ oz butter beans, sliced

100 g/3½ oz broad beans/fava beans, peeled

30 ml/1 fl oz red-wine vinegar

1 teaspoon sea salt

1 teaspoon freshly ground black pepper

½ cup chopped chervil *or* flat-leaf parsley

Chargrilled beef with bean salad and harissa

1 Preheat oven to hot (220°C/450°F). **2** To make bean salad, heat 20 ml/¾ oz of the oil and fry onion, garlic and chilli until beginning to colour. Add cumin and lentils and fry for another minute or two. Add stock and cook over low heat for about 20 minutes, or until lentils are soft and liquid has been absorbed. Remove from heat. **3** Cook green beans, butter beans and broad beans in boiling salted water for 2 minutes, or until al dente. Strain and rinse under cold water to refresh and maintain colour. Add cooked beans to lentils. **4** Whisk vinegar and remaining olive oil in a bowl and season with salt and pepper. Dress beans with vinaigrette and add chervil. **5** To cook beef, rub olive oil and HARISSA over meat to coat thoroughly. Heat a chargrill pan and sear meat on all sides for about 10 minutes, or until browned. Transfer to a baking tray and cook in oven for 8 minutes. At this stage, the meat should be medium–rare, quite pink in the centre and maintaining maximum moisture. Remove from oven and rest for 10 minutes before slicing. **6** Spoon bean salad onto a large plate. Slice beef and arrange on top of salad. Serve with extra HARISSA and crusty bread.

Serves 4

Note: Instead of chargrilling, the meat can be barbecued over hot coals for 10–15 minutes and then rested in a warm place for 15 minutes.

Sambal Bajak

By their very nature, all sambals should be slightly fiery on the palate. Because it is a cooked preparation, this sambal is more gentle, relatively speaking, than the raw varieties (sambal olek) that are commercially available. Sambal bajak includes onions for sweetness and shrimp paste and tamarind for sourness and depth of flavour. Used mainly in Indonesian cooking and popular with rice dishes such as Nasi Goreng, it is made with the milder, large Lombok or Chinese chillies. Any sambal preparation can be served as a condiment or an accompaniment to a main dish, where its piquancy lifts the flavour of the food. Having a range of sambals at hand means that you can transform ordinary food in a flash. Like CHILLI JAM, this sambal is partnered by and compatible with other pastes throughout this book.

Sambal bajak

30 g/1 oz Malaysian shrimp paste/belacan
20 large red Chinese *or* Dutch chillies, chopped
6 candlenuts
4 teaspoons finely chopped ginger
4 teaspoons finely chopped garlic
10 red shallots, sliced
6 kaffir lime leaves, shredded
50 ml/1½ fl oz vegetable oil
30 ml/1 fl oz Tamarind Liquid (page 200)
250 ml/8 fl oz coconut milk
30 g/1 oz palm sugar/jaggery, shaved
40 ml/1¼ fl oz fish sauce

1 Dry-roast shrimp paste over gentle heat until fragrant. Blend shrimp paste, chilli, candlenuts, ginger, garlic, shallots, lime leaves and oil to a smooth paste in a food processor. **2** Cook paste over gentle heat for 10–15 minutes, or until softened. Add remaining ingredients and bring to the boil. Simmer for 30 minutes until a thick paste has formed and a layer of oil is evident. **3** Stir oil back into sambal and remove from heat. Spoon into a sterilised jar and seal when cool. Keeps, refrigerated, for up to 2 months.
Makes about 300 ml/10 fl oz

½ tablespoon raw peanuts

1 teaspoon chilli oil

½ clove garlic, sliced

½ teaspoon finely chopped ginger

¼ large red Chinese *or* Dutch chilli, cut into julienne

¼ red capsicum/bell pepper, cut into julienne

½ green onion/scallion, cut into 2.5 cm/1 in lengths

¼ small carrot, cut into julienne

¼ zucchini/courgette, cut into julienne

2 snow peas, cut into julienne

½ snake bean, cut into 5 cm/2 in lengths and blanched

2 oyster mushrooms, halved

½ Chinese cabbage/bai choy leaf, coarsely shredded

30 g/1 oz bean sprouts

20 ml/¾ fl oz Tamarind Liquid (page 200)

½ teaspoon sugar

½ teaspoon fish sauce

1 teaspoon sweet soy sauce/kecap manis

1 teaspoon SAMBAL BAJAK (page 42)

½ cup small tatsoi leaves *or* watercress sprigs

½ large hard-boiled egg

Stir-fried chilli vegetables with roasted peanuts

1 Dry-roast peanuts over low heat until coloured and fragrant. Cool and chop roughly. Set aside. **2** Heat a wok, add chilli oil and fry garlic, ginger and chilli for 1 minute, or until fragrant. Add capsicum, green onion, carrot, zucchini, snow peas, snake bean and mushrooms and toss over heat for 1–2 minutes, or until vegetables start to wilt. Add cabbage and bean sprouts with tamarind liquid, sugar, fish sauce, soy sauce and SAMBAL BAJAK. Toss to combine. Stir tatsoi through hot vegetables and remove wok from heat. **3** Pile stir-fried vegetables on a plate, top with egg and sprinkle with roasted peanuts. Serve immediately.

Serves 1

Note: If making this dish for more than 1 person, cook each serving separately for best results.

20 ml/¾ fl oz vegetable oil

2 cloves garlic, finely chopped

1 small red birds-eye *or* serrano chilli, finely chopped

2 teaspoons fish sauce

4 teaspoons Chinese oyster sauce

2 teaspoons Chinese black vinegar

1 teaspoon sweet soy sauce/kecap manis

200 g/6½ oz green beans, trimmed

4 teaspoons SAMBAL BAJAK (page 42)

4 green onions/scallions, finely sliced

Green bean sambal

1 Heat oil in a wok, add garlic, chilli, fish sauce, oyster sauce, vinegar, sweet soy sauce and green beans. Toss over heat and cook for 2 minutes, or until beans begin to soften. **2** Stir in SAMBAL BAJAK and cook for another minute to coat beans with paste. Add a little water to prevent burning. **3** Remove from heat, add sliced green onion and serve.

Serves 4

Note: Thin asparagus can be substituted for beans.

Spiced coconut fish soup

20 ml/¾ fl oz vegetable oil

2 stalks lemongrass, chopped

4 kaffir lime leaves, chopped

rind/zest of 2 limes

2 small red birds-eye *or* serrano chillies, sliced

3 teaspoons finely chopped ginger

2 coriander/cilantro/Chinese parsley roots, finely chopped

4 green onions/scallions, sliced

4 teaspoons SAMBAL BAJAK (page 42)

400 ml/12½ fl oz Fish Stock (page 201)

800 ml/26 fl oz coconut milk

2 teaspoons strained lime juice

20 ml/¾ fl oz fish sauce

200 g/6½ oz fish fillets, cut into chunks

¼ cup fresh coriander/cilantro/Chinese parsley leaves

¼ cup shredded mint leaves

1 Heat oil in a pot and fry lemongrass, lime leaves, half the lime rind, chilli, ginger, coriander root and green onion for about 4 minutes, or until softened. Add SAMBAL BAJAK and fry for another minute. Add stock and coconut milk and bring to the boil. Reduce heat and simmer for 20 minutes. **2** Strain soup through a fine mesh sieve, discarding solids. Return soup to pot and flavour with lime juice and fish sauce. **3** Poach fish chunks in soup over gentle heat for 3 minutes. Ladle fish and soup into bowls and add remaining lime rind, coriander leaves and mint leaves.

Serves 4

Note: For variety, use Prawn/Shrimp Stock (page 202) in place of Fish Stock and add shellfish to the broth as well as some fish.

3 tablespoons plain/all-purpose flour
½ teaspoon sea salt
½ teaspoon freshly ground black pepper
½ teaspoon ground chilli *or* paprika
600 g/1 lb 3 oz fresh whitebait, washed and
   dried on paper towel
vegetable oil, for deep-frying
8 teaspoons SAMBAL BAJAK (page 42)
4 lemon wedges

Fried whitebait with chilli

1 Season flour with salt, pepper and chilli. Coat whitebait with seasoned flour. **2** Heat oil to 180°C/350°F in deep-fryer or large pot. Cook whitebait in small batches for 1 minute, or until crisp. Drain on paper towel. **3** Serve with SAMBAL BAJAK and lemon wedges.

Serves 4

40 ml/1¼ fl oz vegetable oil
2 cloves garlic, finely chopped
8 teaspoons SAMBAL BAJAK (page 42)
1 kg/2 lb small green prawns/shrimp (harbour *or*
school prawns *or* shrimp), washed (see Note)

Chilli prawns

1 Heat oil in a wok and fry garlic and SAMBAL BAJAK for a minute. **2** Add prawns and toss over high heat to coat them with chilli. Cook until prawns are crisp and have changed to a bright pink colour. Serve immediately. These prawns are meant to be devoured in their entirety, heads and all. Have an ample supply of napkins on hand.

Serves 4

Note: Larger prawns can be used in this recipe, but discard the heads before cooking and remove the tough shells before eating.

20 ml/¾ fl oz strained lime juice

½ teaspoon freshly ground white pepper

4 teaspoons SAMBAL BAJAK (page 42)

16 green king *or* tiger prawns/shrimp, shelled
    and deveined

2 teaspoons vegetable oil

125 ml/4 fl oz coconut cream

2 teaspoons fish sauce

1 tablespoon finely shredded mint leaves

2 teaspoons Fried Shallot Slices (page 201)

Prawn sambal

1 Combine lime juice, pepper and SAMBAL BAJAK in a bowl. Add prawns and coat thoroughly with paste. **2** Heat oil in a wok or heavy-based pan and fry prawns over moderately high heat for 2 minutes to seal in juices. **3** Add coconut cream and fish sauce and stir to combine. Cook for 2 minutes only. **4** Remove from heat, garnish with shredded mint and fried shallot slices and serve with salad or rice.

Serves 4

400 g/12½ oz cleaned squid tubes
4 teaspoons SAMBAL BAJAK (page 42)
2 teaspoons strained lime juice
2 teaspoons fish sauce
20 ml/¾ fl oz vegetable oil
80 ml/2½ fl oz Sweet Chilli Sauce (page 200)
1 small cucumber, finely sliced
150 g/5 oz bean sprouts
2 green onions/scallions, finely sliced
¼ cup shredded mint leaves
¼ cup coriander/cilantro/Chinese parsley leaves
1 large red Chinese *or* Dutch chilli, finely sliced

Chilli squid salad

1 Cut squid tubes in half lengthwise and carefully score inner flesh diagonally. Combine squid, SAMBAL BAJAK, lime juice and fish sauce in a bowl. **2** Heat oil in a wok or pan and fry squid over high heat for 2 minutes, or until just cooked. It will curl as it cooks because of the scoring, which also helps to keep it tender. **3** Remove from heat, toss with sweet chilli sauce and remaining salad ingredients and serve.

Serves 4

Note: Cuttlefish or small octopus can just as easily be used in this preparation.

4 tablespoons SAMBAL BAJAK (page 42)

4 fresh banana leaves, cut into large squares

4 × 150 g/5 oz white fish fillets (snapper, blue eye,
   rock cod, barramundi, bream etc.)

½ teaspoon sea salt

½ teaspoon freshly ground black pepper

40 ml/1¼ fl oz strained lime juice

green onions/scallions, finely sliced

slices of lime

steamed rice, to serve

Chilli fish baked in banana leaf

1 Spoon 2 teaspoons SAMBAL BAJAK onto each banana leaf. Lay each fish fillet on a banana leaf and season with salt, pepper and lime juice. Spoon remaining SAMBAL BAJAK over fish and fold banana leaf over to cover the fish and make a package. Secure with skewers or toothpicks. **2** Cook fish parcels over a charcoal grill or in a moderate (180°C/350°F) oven for 5–6 minutes each side (10–12 minutes total, or longer if necessary, depending on the thickness and density of the fish). **3** Remove fish parcels from heat, unwrap and discard banana leaves. Scatter green onion over the fish and add a slice or two of lime, if desired. Serve with steamed rice.

Serves 4

Chilli soy chicken with sesame noodles

2 teaspoons white sesame seeds

vegetable oil

8 cloves garlic

3 litres/96 fl oz Red Braising Stock (page 203)

4 chicken thighs, cut in half at the joint

1 teaspoon Sichuan Spice Salt (page 200)

4 Japanese/Asian eggplants/aubergines

250 g/8 oz somen noodles

¼ cup shredded spearmint leaves

2 tablespoons torn basil leaves

2 green onions/scallions, finely sliced

2 cups watercress sprigs

Sesame soy dressing

40 ml/1¼ fl oz soy sauce

2 teaspoons sesame oil

4 teaspoons SAMBAL BAJAK (page 42)

40 ml/1¼ fl oz lemon juice, strained

50 ml/1½ fl oz Chinese rice vinegar

60 ml/2 fl oz mirin

60 ml/2 fl oz Sugar Syrup (page 201) *or*

   2 tablespoons caster sugar

4 cloves garlic, finely chopped

1 Dry-roast sesame seeds in a frying pan over gentle heat until just coloured. Cool and set aside. **2** Heat oil and shallow-fry garlic cloves until golden and softened. Drain on paper towel. **3** To make dressing, combine all ingredients. Set aside. **4** Bring stock to the boil in a stockpot. Put chicken pieces into stock, turn off heat and let chicken cook gently in hot stock for 30 minutes. Check that meat is cooked by testing each piece with a skewer – if juices run pale pink, chicken is ready. Leave a little longer if juices are too pink. **5** Remove cooked chicken from stock and cut meat into strips or shred with fingers, discarding bones. Sprinkle with Sichuan spice salt. **6** Quarter eggplants lengthwise, score flesh and brush with oil. Grill until softened and golden brown. **7** Cook noodles in boiling water for 2 minutes, or until soft. Drain and refresh under cold running water. Put noodles into a bowl with half the dressing. **8** In another bowl, mix garlic with herbs, green onion and watercress. Add chicken and spoon in enough dressing to coat leaves and meat lightly. **9** Pile noodles on plates and sit 2 grilled eggplant halves on each serving. Arrange chicken and salad on top of eggplant and drizzle with a little extra dressing. Sprinkle with sesame seeds and serve immediately.

Serves 4

vegetable oil, for deep-frying
1 kg/2 lb pork spareribs, trimmed and cut into
   single ribs, on the bone
1 litre/32 fl oz White Chicken Stock (page 202)
4 cloves garlic, finely chopped
4 slices ginger
4 green onions/scallions, chopped
8 teaspoons SAMBAL BAJAK (page 42)
20 ml/¾ fl oz Chinese yellow bean sauce
20 ml/¾ fl oz light soy sauce
2 teaspoons sweet soy sauce/kecap manis
1 tablespoon shaved palm sugar/jaggery
40 ml/1¼ fl oz Chinese Shaoxing rice wine
2 teaspoons fish sauce
steamed Chinese broccoli/gai lan, to serve

Chilli pork spareribs

1 Heat oil to 180°C/350°F in a deep-fryer or large pot and deep-fry spareribs, a few at a time, for 5 minutes until brown. Drain on paper towel. **2** Heat stock with remaining ingredients, except Chinese broccoli, to boiling point in a large saucepan. Reduce heat to a simmer, add spareribs and simmer over low heat for 1 hour. **3** Preheat oven to moderately hot (200°C/400°F). Remove ribs from stock and lay on a wire rack placed over a roasting tray. Bake for 10 minutes, or until crisp. Serve with Chinese broccoli and extra SAMBAL BAJAK as a condiment.

Serves 4

50 g/1½ oz dried rice vermicelli/beehoon

24 cooked yabby tails, peeled (see Note)

12 × 16 cm/6 in square rice paper sheets

1 cup bean sprouts, blanched

½ cup snow pea sprouts

2 tablespoons finely grated carrot

2 tablespoons shredded cucumber

2 tablespoons Vietnamese mint/laksa leaves

2 tablespoons coriander/cilantro/Chinese parsley leaves

4 teaspoons SAMBAL BAJAK (page 42)

Sweet chilli and peanut dipping sauce

125 ml/4 fl oz lime juice

60 ml/2 fl oz fish sauce

40 ml/1¼ fl oz rice vinegar *or* coconut vinegar

3 tablespoons caster sugar

2 cloves garlic, minced

2 red birds-eye chillies, minced

1 tablespoon crushed roasted peanuts

Rice paper rolls with yabbies and chilli

1 To make the dipping sauce, combine all ingredients except peanuts. Taste and adjust seasoning if necessary. Set aside. **2** Soak vermicelli in warm water for 30 minutes, then cook in boiling water for 2 minutes or until soft. Drain and refresh with cold water. Drain again and set aside. Cut yabby tails in half lengthwise and devein. **3** Set out all ingredients on work surface, with a large bowl of hot water alongside. Lay a clean, folded tea towel next to the bowl. **4** Working with 1 sheet of rice paper at a time, soften each sheet in hot water for 30 seconds. Lift from water and place on folded cloth. Lay a few vermicelli noodles on rice paper, about a third up from base and spreading them two-thirds of the way across the sheet. **5** On top of noodles, place bean sprouts, snow pea sprouts, carrot and cucumber, then Vietnamese mint and coriander leaves. Lay 4 yabby tail halves along the top and spread with a little SAMBAL BAJAK. **6** Roll sheet over filling, carefully tucking in the ends to secure. Roll over firmly to make neat, uniform rolls. As you complete each roll, set it on a plate, seam-side down. Continue until all ingredients have been used. **7** Add crushed peanuts to dipping sauce and serve rolls immediately with sauce.

Makes 12

Note: If yabby tails are not available, use prawns, crayfish or lobster tails, scampi or even freshly picked crabmeat.

Spiced Eggplant Pickle

I have read somewhere that the people of India refer to their pickles and chutneys as 'tongue touchers', which I think is a most apt description, evocative of their nature and necessity for inclusion in the ritual of everyday eating. Pickles – cooked preparations where vegetables or fruit are sharpened with vinegar and made fiery with assorted spices – give unparalleled diversity and sensuality to food. For those who appreciate the taste of preserves, this rich, vibrant and spicy pickle is an absolute essential in the larder. It can be served with curries, dosas (rice pancakes) or parathas (flaky Indian bread), or as an accompaniment to cold meats, grilled fish or seafood. It can also be used as a base for other preparations. A small quantity can go a long way.

6 large dried Chinese *or* Dutch chillies
4 teaspoons finely chopped garlic
2 teaspoons finely chopped ginger
1 teaspoon ground turmeric
4 teaspoons brown mustard seeds
500 g/1 lb small eggplants/aubergines, washed
200 ml/6½ fl oz vegetable oil
60 g/2 oz palm sugar/jaggery, shaved
2 teaspoons sea salt
100 ml/3½ fl oz malt vinegar
1 teaspoon Garam Masala (page 200)

Spiced eggplant pickle

1 Soak chillies in hot water for about 30 minutes, or until soft. Drain, reserving water. In a food processor, blend chillies, garlic, ginger, turmeric and mustard seeds to a paste with a little reserved soaking water. **2** Slice eggplants into rounds 1 cm/½ in thick. **3** Heat oil in a frying pan, then add spice paste and stir for a few minutes to release flavours. Add eggplant and cook, stirring occasionally, until soft. Add palm sugar, salt and vinegar and simmer over low heat until thick. Remove from heat and stir in garam masala. Cool. **4** Spoon into sterilised jars, cover with a film of oil and seal. Keeps, refrigerated, for 2 months.

Makes about 500 ml/16 fl oz

ghee

½ teaspoon brown mustard seeds

20 fresh curry leaves

2 large dried Kashmiri, Chinese *or* New Mexican red chillies

2 small brown onions, finely sliced

1 teaspoon finely chopped ginger

2 small red birds-eye *or* serrano chillies, split lengthwise

4 teaspoons mild curry powder

1 teaspoon ground turmeric

200 ml/6½ fl oz coconut milk

200 ml/6½ fl oz water

400 g/12½ oz potatoes, peeled and cut into 2.5 cm/1 in dice

3 tomatoes, peeled and quartered

4 tablespoons cooked peas

1 teaspoon sea salt

8 teaspoons SPICED EGGPLANT PICKLE (page 60)

Coconut flatbread

300 g/9½ oz plain/all-purpose flour

2 tablespoons rice flour

250 ml/8 fl oz lukewarm water

2 tablespoons desiccated coconut

1 teaspoon finely chopped green jalapeño chilli

2 teaspoons finely chopped ginger

1 teaspoon sea salt

Potato curry with Indian-style flatbread and spiced eggplant pickle

1 Heat 1 tablespoon ghee in a pan and cook mustard seeds, curry leaves and dried chillies for 30 seconds, or until seeds pop. Stir in onion, ginger and fresh chilli and cook for about 2 minutes, or until softened. Add curry powder and turmeric and stir to coat onion. Pour in coconut milk and water and bring to a simmer. **2** Add potato and tomato and cook over low heat for 20 minutes, or until potato is soft. Add peas and season to taste with salt. Remove from heat and reheat gently when ready to serve. **3** To make flatbread, sift flours into a bowl. Slowly stir in water to make a smooth batter. Mix in coconut, chilli, ginger and salt. **4** Heat a flat griddle or frying pan, add a little ghee and pour in enough batter to cover base, turning pan to coat base evenly. Cook flatbread over moderate heat for 3–4 minutes, then flip over and cook the other side for another 3 minutes, or until golden. Repeat process until all batter is used. **5** Serve hot flatbread and curry with SPICED EGGPLANT PICKLE as a condiment.

Serves 4

Note: If you don't have time to make the flatbread, order some naan bread or parathas from your nearest Indian takeaway, or serve the curry and pickle with rice and pappadams. This preparation is known as Masala Dosa.

500 ml/16 fl oz thick plain yoghurt
vegetable oil, for deep-frying
2 eggplants/aubergines, cut into 1 cm/½ in dice
8 teaspoons SPICED EGGPLANT PICKLE (page 60)
2 teaspoons fish sauce
¼ cup chopped coriander/cilantro/Chinese parsley leaves

Spiced eggplant pickle and yoghurt salad

1 Spoon yoghurt into a strainer lined with cheesecloth and hang overnight to remove excess moisture. **2** To prepare salad, heat oil to 180°C/350°F in a deep-fryer or large pot and fry eggplant until golden. Drain on paper towel. **3** Mix eggplant in a bowl with remaining ingredients. Cover and refrigerate until ready to use. Serve with prawn or vegetable pakoras/fritters or with grilled spicy fish fillets, or wrap in flatbread (mountain bread, soft tortilla, Lebanese or Turkish bread) with grilled lamb or chicken as a variation to a regular luncheon sandwich.

Serves 4

Pumpkin and pickled eggplant samosas

10 × 20 cm/8 in square spring roll wrappers
1 egg white
vegetable oil, for deep-frying
Filling
2 tablespoons ghee
2 cloves garlic, finely chopped
1 teaspoon finely chopped ginger
2 small red birds-eye *or* serrano chillies, finely chopped
200 g/6½ oz pumpkin, cut into 6 mm/¼ in dice
200 g/6½ oz eggplants/aubergines, cut into 6 mm/¼ in dice
2 teaspoons sea salt
8 teaspoons SPICED EGGPLANT PICKLE (page 60)
2 tablespoons chopped coriander/cilantro/
   Chinese parsley leaves

1 To make filling, heat ghee in a frying pan over moderate heat and cook garlic, ginger and chilli for 1 minute. Add pumpkin and eggplant and cook for another 8–10 minutes, or until pumpkin has softened. Season to taste with salt and stir in SPICED EGGPLANT PICKLE. Remove from heat, allow mixture to cool, then add coriander. **2** To assemble pastries, cut each wrapper into 3 strips lengthwise, giving you 30 rectangular strips. Place 1 large teaspoon of filling mixture on bottom left corner of each strip and fold over and over to wrap into a triangular shape. Brush the last 6 mm/¼ in of pastry with egg white and seal. Lay prepared pastries on a tray in a single layer until ready to cook. **3** To cook pastries, heat vegetable oil to 180°C/350°F in a deep-fryer or large pot and fry, a few at a time, for 4 minutes or until crisp and golden. Remove from oil with a slotted spoon and drain on paper towel. Serve hot with a yoghurt-based dipping sauce.

Makes 30

4 chicken thigh fillets, skin removed
1 teaspoon Garam Masala (page 200)
2 cloves garlic, minced
20 ml/¾ fl oz lime juice
1 teaspoon sea salt
1 teaspoon freshly ground black pepper
40 ml/1¼ fl oz vegetable oil
4 flatbreads (see Note)
4 teaspoons SPICED EGGPLANT PICKLE (page 60)
1 small cucumber, seeded and finely diced
1 small red onion, finely diced
200 g/6½ oz thick plain yoghurt
2 tablespoons shredded mint

Chicken kebab and eggplant pickle wraps

1 Soak 8 wooden skewers in water for 1 hour (to prevent them burning during cooking). **2** Cut chicken into 3 cm/1¼ in cubes. Mix garam masala, garlic, lime juice, salt and pepper with oil. Marinate chicken in spiced oil for 30 minutes before cooking. **3** Thread chicken cubes onto skewers. Cook for 5 minutes over hot coals on a barbecue or on a hot grill plate. Carefully turn skewers over and cook for a further 3–4 minutes or until chicken is cooked and tender. Remove from heat. **4** Grill flatbreads for 2 minutes or until warm and softened. Lay on work surface and spread with eggplant pickle. Remove chicken from skewers and arrange down centre of bread (2 skewers per flatbread). Add cucumber and onion. Spoon over some yoghurt and sprinkle with mint. Wrap breads up and serve immediately.

Serves 4

Note: Any flatbread will do for this dish – pita, roti, naan, lavash, enchilada or tortilla. Use whichever you prefer and have easy access to.

Laksa Paste

While we may all be familiar with laksa as a soup, we may not be fully aware of the different varieties that are on offer at the source or home of origin. These soups can be based on coconut milk like those from Malacca, or tamarind like those of Penang or Ipoh. The characteristics of a laksa change according to how it is made, the type of noodles used and the ingredients that are added for serving. A flavoursome stock is as important as the quality of the laksa paste. From there, you can create culinary nirvana. This delicious, addictive paste is an absolute essential in your pantry. Originating in Malaysia and of Nonya origin, its authentic flavour is second to none. It can also be used as a stir-fry paste, a marinade for grilled foods or a curry paste, or it can be added to pickles or chutneys for greater depth of flavour.

Laksa paste

5 g/⅛ oz dried birds-eye chillies
60 g/2 oz Malaysian shrimp paste/belacan
20 g/¾ oz dried prawns/shrimp
15 g/½ oz ground turmeric
10 g/⅓ oz coriander seeds, roasted and ground
125 g/4 oz fresh lemongrass stalks, finely sliced
90 g/3 oz fresh galangal, chopped
75 g/2½ oz fresh turmeric, chopped
50 g/1½ oz red birds-eye chillies
150 g/5 oz golden shallots, finely sliced
150 g/5 oz cloves garlic
100 g/3½ oz candlenuts *or* macadamia nuts
500 ml/16 fl oz light olive oil

1 Dry-roast dried chillies and shrimp paste separately over low heat until fragrant. **2** Soak dried prawns in warm water for 10 minutes, then drain. **3** Blend all ingredients to a fine paste in a food processor or blender, adding a little water if necessary. **4** Heat a wok and gently fry paste over moderate heat, stirring frequently, for 10–15 minutes or until oil takes on a red colour and the mixture is fragrant and thick. **5** Spoon into sterilised jars and seal when cool. Keeps, refrigerated, for 1 month.

Makes about 600 ml/20 fl oz

625 ml/20 fl oz coconut milk

8 teaspoons LAKSA PASTE (page 68)

4 teaspoons tomato purée

1 teaspoon CHILLI JAM (page 6)

625 ml/20 fl oz Spiced Vegetable Stock (page 204)

3 teaspoons strained lime juice

20 ml/¾ fl oz fish sauce

300 g/9½ oz Chinese egg noodles

200 g/6½ oz rice vermicelli/beehoon, soaked until soft

4 fresh beancurd/tofu squares, deep-fried and cut in half

8 oyster mushrooms, halved

8 snow peas, sliced in half lengthwise

4 tablespoons snow pea sprouts, trimmed

125 g/4 oz bean sprouts

3 kaffir lime leaves, shredded

2 hard-boiled eggs, sliced in half lengthwise

4 teaspoons coriander/cilantro/Chinese parsley leaves

4 teaspoons Vietnamese mint/laksa leaves

2 small red birds-eye *or* serrano chillies, finely sliced
  into rounds

4 teaspoons Fried Shallot Slices (page 201)

4 lime wedges

Spicy vegetable laksa

1 Bring coconut milk, LAKSA PASTE, tomato purée and CHILLI JAM slowly to the boil, uncovered, in a saucepan. Reduce heat and simmer for 5 minutes, or until oil rises to surface. **2** Add stock and return to the boil, uncovered. Reduce heat and simmer gently for 10 minutes. Season with lime juice and fish sauce. Taste and, if necessary, adjust seasoning. **3** Scald both types of noodles in boiling water, drain and divide between 4 bowls. Toss beancurd, mushrooms, snow peas, snow pea sprouts, bean sprouts and lime leaves over noodles. **4** Ladle soup into bowls over vegetables and noodles. Top with sliced egg, coriander and Vietnamese mint leaves, sliced chilli and fried shallot slices and serve with a lime wedge.

Serves 4

20 ml/¾ fl oz light soy sauce

1 teaspoon sesame oil

½ teaspoon freshly ground white pepper

4 × 150 g/5 oz white fish fillets

2 tablespoons Fried Shallot Slices (page 201)

Laksa sauce

20 ml/¾ fl oz vegetable oil

8 teaspoons LAKSA PASTE (page 68)

1 stalk lemongrass, roughly chopped

2 small red birds-eye *or* Thai *or* serrano chillies, chopped

2 kaffir lime leaves

200 ml/6½ fl oz coconut cream

4 teaspoons tomato purée

250 ml/8 fl oz Fish Stock (page 201)

2 teaspoons fish sauce

1 teaspoon strained lime juice

Steamed fish with laksa sauce

1 To make laksa sauce, heat oil in pan and fry LAKSA PASTE with lemongrass, chilli and lime leaves for about 5 minutes, or until fragrant. **2** Add coconut cream and tomato purée and bring to simmering point. Cook on gentle heat for 5 minutes, then add stock. Simmer for 20 minutes, then add fish sauce and lime juice. If sauce gets too thick, add a little extra fish stock. Taste and, if necessary, adjust seasoning. **3** Remove from heat and pour sauce through a fine mesh sieve or muslin. Discard solids. Sauce can be made ahead of time and gently reheated when ready to serve. **4** Combine soy sauce, sesame oil and pepper and brush onto fish fillets. Lay fillets on a plate and place in a steamer tray over gently boiling water. Cover with a lid and steam for 6–10 minutes, depending on size and thickness of fish fillets. Test centre of fillets with a skewer. Flesh should be white and firm without being dry or breaking open. **5** Place steamed fish on laksa sauce and top with fried shallot slices. Serve with preferred accompaniment – steamed Chinese broccoli/gai lan or another green leafy vegetable, steamed jasmine rice, roasted tomatoes or noodles.

Serves 4

Note: Any white fish can be used for this dish.

Stir-fried lemon prawns and squid

12 green king prawns/shrimp
8 small squid, cleaned
40 ml/1¼ fl oz vegetable oil
1 teaspoon sesame oil
4 red shallots, finely sliced
2 cloves garlic, finely sliced
2 large red Chinese *or* Dutch chillies, finely sliced
8 teaspoons LAKSA PASTE (page 68)
3 teaspoons fish sauce
50 ml/1½ fl oz lemon juice
100 g/3½ oz snow pea sprouts
½ cup lemon basil *or* basil leaves
steamed rice, to serve

1 Peel and devein prawns, leaving tails intact. Cut squid tubes into thick strips lengthwise and carefully score inner flesh diagonally. **2** Heat both oils in a wok and fry shallots, garlic and chilli over high heat for 30 seconds. Add LAKSA PASTE, fish sauce and lemon juice and fry for another minute or so until fragrant. **3** Add prawns and squid (tentacles, too, if desired) and toss over high heat for 2 minutes, or until just cooked. Stir to ensure seafood is evenly coated with spice paste. **4** Add snow pea sprouts and toss over heat for another minute. **5** Remove from heat, stir through basil leaves and serve with steamed rice.
Serves 4

Hot-and-sour fish soup

2 teaspoons vegetable oil
1 small onion, chopped
8 teaspoons LAKSA PASTE (page 68)
1.5 litres/48 fl oz Fish Stock (page 201) *or* water
200 ml/6½ fl oz Tamarind Liquid (page 200)
20 ml/¾ fl oz fish sauce
8 Chinese cabbage/bai choy leaves, shredded
2 tomatoes, peeled and chopped
100 g/3½ oz snake beans, cut into 5 cm/2 in lengths
kernels from 2 cobs of corn
12 straw mushrooms, cut in half lengthwise
extra vegetable oil, for deep-frying
4 × 75 g/2½ oz fish fillets
2 cups cooked rice
¼ cup coriander/cilantro/Chinese parsley leaves

1 Heat oil in a saucepan and fry onion and LAKSA PASTE for a few minutes, or until fragrant. Add stock, tamarind liquid and fish sauce and bring to the boil. Reduce heat and simmer for 10 minutes. **2** Add vegetables and cook for 20 minutes, or until vegetables are very soft. Taste and, if necessary, adjust seasoning. **3** Heat oil in a deep-fryer or saucepan and fry fish fillets for 6–8 minutes, or until very crisp. Remove from oil and drain on paper towel. **4** Divide cooked rice between 4 bowls and ladle hot soup over. Top with fried fish and coriander leaves.

Serves 4

2 chicken breasts, skin removed
500 ml/16 fl oz White Chicken Stock (page 202)
250 ml/8 fl oz coconut cream
8 teaspoons LAKSA PASTE (page 68)
1 teaspoon CHILLI JAM (page 6)
500 ml/16 fl oz coconut milk
2 teaspoons strained lime juice
20 ml/¾ fl oz fish sauce
500 g/1 lb fresh rice noodles
2 kaffir lime leaves, finely shredded
125 g/4 oz bean sprouts
1 small cucumber, peeled, seeded and shredded
2 teaspoons Fried Shallot Slices (page 201)
1 tablespoon coriander/cilantro/Chinese parsley leaves
2 small red birds-eye *or* serrano chillies, finely sliced
16 Vietnamese mint/laksa leaves

Coconut chicken laksa

1 Steam or poach chicken gently in stock for 15 minutes, or until just cooked through. Remove chicken from stock and cool. Shred meat. Reserve stock. **2** Bring coconut cream, LAKSA PASTE and CHILLI JAM slowly to the boil, uncovered, in a saucepan. Reduce heat and simmer for 10 minutes, or until oil rises to surface. **3** Add coconut milk and stock and return to the boil, uncovered. Reduce heat and simmer gently for 15 minutes. Season with lime juice and fish sauce. Taste and, if necessary, adjust seasoning. **4** Put noodles and chicken into separate noodle baskets or conical sieves and lower into soup for about 20 seconds, or until warmed through. **5** Divide noodles and chicken between 4 bowls and add lime leaves and bean sprouts. Ladle soup into each bowl to cover noodles and stir with a chopstick to combine. Sprinkle remaining ingredients over and serve immediately.

Serves 4

Margie's five-minute noodles

1 teaspoon LAKSA PASTE (page 68)
1 teaspoon CHILLI JAM (page 6)
1 teaspoon fish sauce
20 ml/¾ fl oz water
1 teaspoon sweet soy sauce/kecap manis
100 g/3½ oz fresh rice noodle sheets, cut into
    thick ribbons
handful of tatsoi *or* baby spinach leaves
50 g/1½ oz cooked chicken, shredded
2 teaspoons Thai/holy basil leaves
2 teaspoons coriander/cilantro/Chinese parsley leaves

1 Mix LAKSA PASTE with CHILLI JAM. Heat a wok and dry-fry paste for 1 minute, or until fragrant. **2** Add fish sauce, water and soy sauce and toss to combine. **3** Add rice noodles and toss over high heat to coat noodles with paste. Cook for 1 minute, or until noodles begin to soften. **4** Add tatsoi, chicken and basil and continue to toss over high heat for 1 minute, or until chicken is heated through. **5** Remove from heat and add coriander leaves. Taste and, if necessary, adjust seasoning. Serve immediately.

Serves 1

Note: If you are making this dish for more than 1 person, cook each serving separately in a wok for best results.

Spiced quails with mushrooms

4 small dried birds-eye *or* Thai chillies, roasted and ground
1 teaspoon black peppercorns, ground
2 teaspoons sea salt
6 large quails, cut in half lengthwise
vegetable oil, for deep-frying
extra 20 ml/¾ fl oz vegetable oil
1 medium-size brown onion, finely sliced lengthwise
4 teaspoons LAKSA PASTE (page 68)
12 shiitake mushrooms, sliced
12 straw mushrooms, halved lengthwise
2 tablespoons shredded fresh cloud ear fungus
2 large red Chinese *or* Dutch chillies, finely sliced
3 teaspoons fish sauce
30 ml/1 fl oz sweet soy sauce/kecap manis
12 green beans, sliced
4 tablespoons torn Thai/holy basil leaves

1 Combine ground chilli, pepper and salt and rub into quail halves to season. **2** Heat oil to 180°C/350°F in a deep-fryer or large pot and deep-fry quail, 6 pieces at a time to maintain oil temperature, for 5 minutes or until crisp and just cooked. Remove from oil and drain on paper towel. Repeat until all quail pieces are cooked. Sprinkle quail with a little of the remaining seasoned salt. **3** Heat extra vegetable oil in a wok and fry onion until softened and beginning to colour. Stir in LAKSA PASTE and toss over high heat to combine. **4** Add mushrooms, fungus and chilli and continue to toss over high heat to combine ingredients thoroughly. **5** Add fish sauce and soy sauce, stir, then toss in beans and cook for another minute. **6** Add basil leaves, taste and, if necessary, adjust seasoning. **7** Place stir-fried mushrooms on plates, lay crisp spiced quails on top and serve immediately.

Serves 4

4 × 150 g/5 oz lamb loins *or* backstraps
8 teaspoons LAKSA PASTE (page 68)
20 ml/¾ fl oz vegetable oil
2 tablespoons shredded mint leaves
8 stalks lemongrass, trimmed to 10 cm/4 in lengths
2 bunches thin asparagus
sea salt
freshly ground black pepper
Yoghurt mint salad
¼ cup coriander/cilantro/Chinese parsley leaves, shredded
2 tablespoons shredded spearmint leaves
1 small green jalapeño chilli, finely sliced into rounds
2 red shallots, finely chopped
½ teaspoon finely chopped ginger
2 teaspoons fish sauce
1 teaspoon strained lime juice
200 ml/6½ fl oz thick plain yoghurt
1 cucumber, peeled, seeded and cut into julienne
¼ teaspoon sea salt
¼ teaspoon freshly ground black pepper

Grilled spiced lamb with mint and asparagus

1 Trim lamb of any sinew or fat and cut each loin into 8 cubes. **2** Mix LAKSA PASTE, oil and mint and work into meat. Marinate for 2 hours. Thread 4 lamb cubes onto each lemongrass stalk, keeping the meat pieces close together. **3** Make yoghurt mint salad by mixing ingredients thoroughly in a bowl. Keep refrigerated until ready to serve. **4** Heat a cast-iron grill pan or barbecue and grill lamb kebabs for 12–15 minutes, or until lamb is tender yet still pink in the centre. Remove from heat and rest for a few minutes in a warm place. **5** Trim tough ends from asparagus spears, brush with a little oil and grill until soft and beginning to scorch. Remove from heat and season to taste. **6** Arrange lamb kebabs and grilled asparagus on plates and serve with yoghurt mint salad.

Serves 4

Black Pepper and Lemongrass Stir-fry Paste

Quick and easy stir-frying is so popular these days that you'll want to keep this fragrant and versatile paste in your pantry always. It has a warm, mellow, mid-palate flavour because the black pepper and chilli are tempered by the fresh zing of lemongrass and lime, and it responds perfectly to the intense heat of wok cooking by releasing its flavour and aroma immediately. Use it when you stir-fry, to marinate food to be cooked on the barbecue, to spice up a soup, to toss with noodles in a variety of ways (as you will see in this chapter) or to mix with other chilli pastes for an even more intense flavour hit.

Black pepper and lemongrass stir-fry paste

350 g/11 oz fresh lemongrass stalks
50 g/1½ oz red *or* golden shallots, finely chopped
150 g/5 oz cloves garlic, finely chopped
50 g/1½ oz ginger, finely chopped
20 g/¾ oz coriander/cilantro/Chinese parsley roots,
  finely chopped
10 kaffir lime leaves
50 g/1½ oz red birds-eye chillies, finely chopped
60 ml/2 fl oz chilli oil
20 g/¾ oz coarsely ground black pepper
12 large dried Chinese *or* Dutch chillies,
  dry-roasted and ground
50 g/1½ oz salted black beans
40 g/1¼ oz palm sugar/jaggery, shaved
40 g/1¼ oz Malaysian shrimp paste/belacan,
  dry-roasted
60 ml/2 fl oz light soy sauce
60 ml/2 fl oz fish sauce

1 Chop lemongrass finely with a knife, to make the paste finer when processed. **2** Blend lemongrass, shallots, garlic, ginger, coriander root, lime leaves and fresh chilli with chilli oil to a paste in a food processor or blender, then add remaining ingredients. Process paste until it is quite fine. **3** Cook over low heat for 45 minutes. **4** Taste and, if necessary, adjust seasoning. Spoon into sterilised jars, cover with a film of oil and seal when cool. Keeps, refrigerated, for 1 month.

Makes about 750 ml/24 fl oz

2 cups cold cooked jasmine rice
40 ml/1¼ fl oz vegetable oil
2 eggs, lightly beaten
1 medium-size brown onion, finely sliced lengthwise
4 teaspoons BLACK PEPPER AND LEMONGRASS
    STIR-FRY PASTE (page 82)
4 asparagus spears, cut on the diagonal into
    2 cm/¾ in lengths
2 teaspoons salted black beans, washed
100 g/3½ oz bean sprouts
2 teaspoons fish sauce
2 tablespoons snipped garlic chives
2 tablespoons Fried Garlic Slices (page 201)

Vegetable fried rice

1 Using a fork, separate rice grains (to ensure even cooking). **2** Heat half the oil in a wok and add beaten egg. Cook until set. Turn egg out of wok, roll up and slice finely into shreds. Set aside. **3** Heat remaining oil and fry onion with spice paste over high heat for 2 minutes, or until onion begins to colour. **4** Add asparagus, black beans and bean sprouts and toss to combine. **5** Add shredded egg, rice and fish sauce and stir to combine. Cook over high heat for 1 minute, or until rice is heated through. **6** Remove from heat, sprinkle with garlic chives and fried garlic slices and serve.

Serves 4

Fried eggplant salad

2 × 300 g/9½ oz eggplants/aubergines
sea salt
vegetable oil, for deep-frying
extra 30 ml/1 fl oz vegetable oil
4 teaspoons BLACK PEPPER AND LEMONGRASS
  STIR-FRY PASTE (page 82)
5 fresh black wood fungus, shredded
30 ml/1 fl oz Chinese Shaoxing rice wine
30 ml/1 fl oz rice vinegar
40 ml/1¼ fl oz light soy sauce
30 ml/1 fl oz White Chicken Stock (page 202) *or* water
2 teaspoons fish sauce
2 teaspoons caster sugar
1 teaspoon sesame oil
4 green onions/scallions, finely sliced into rounds
½ cup coriander/cilantro/Chinese parsley leaves

1 Quarter eggplants lengthwise, then cut each quarter across into slices 2.5 cm/1 in thick. Sprinkle with salt and place on paper towel in a single layer for 30 minutes. **2** Heat vegetable oil in a deep-fryer or large pot to 180°C/350°F. Blot salt and moisture from eggplant slices with paper towel, then deep-fry in small batches until golden. Drain on paper towel. **3** Heat a large wok and add extra vegetable oil. Toss in spice paste and stir-fry quickly. Add fungus and fried eggplant and toss well. Immediately add rice wine, vinegar, soy sauce, stock, fish sauce and caster sugar and bring to the boil over high heat. This will take 1–2 minutes at most. **4** Reduce heat and simmer for 2 minutes to allow eggplant to absorb some of the liquid. **5** Remove wok from heat and stir in sesame oil, green onion and coriander leaves. Serve immediately.

Serves 4

4 large eggs
20 ml/¾ fl oz vegetable oil
4 teaspoons BLACK PEPPER AND LEMONGRASS
   STIR-FRY PASTE (page 82)
2 teaspoons CHILLI JAM (page 6)
250 ml/8 fl oz coconut milk
2 teaspoons fish sauce
2 teaspoons strained lime juice
¼ cup Fried Shallot Slices (page 201)

Spiced eggs

1 Put eggs in a saucepan of cold water and bring to the boil, stirring occasionally. Boil for 6 minutes. Remove from heat and plunge into cold water. When cool, peel carefully. **2** Heat oil in a saucepan and cook spice paste with CHILLI JAM for 2–3 minutes over moderate heat. **3** When paste starts to smell fragrant, stir in coconut milk and bring to a simmer. Add fish sauce and lime juice and simmer for 10 minutes. **4** Add eggs and cook for 15 minutes, or until sauce thickens, stirring regularly to keep eggs coated with sauce. **5** Remove from heat. Taste and, if necessary, adjust seasoning. Spoon eggs and sauce into a serving bowl and sprinkle with fried shallot slices. Serve as part of a multi-dish feast, including rice.

Serves 4

12 large green tiger *or* king prawns/shrimp
1 tablespoon chopped coriander/cilantro/
    Chinese parsley leaves
6 teaspoons BLACK PEPPER AND LEMONGRASS
    STIR-FRY PASTE (page 82)
12 × 11 cm/4½ in square spring roll wrappers
1 egg white
vegetable oil, for deep-frying
Sweet Chilli Sauce (page 200) *or* Chinese red vinegar
    with ginger

Spiced prawn spring rolls

1 Peel prawns, leaving tails intact. Devein, then butterfly prawns open. **2** Add coriander leaves to spice paste and brush liberally over prawns. **3** Position 1 prawn on each spring roll wrapper with tail hanging over edge. Roll up securely, tucking edges in as you go. Brush wrapper edges with egg white and seal. **4** Heat vegetable oil in a deep-fryer or large pot to 180°C/350°F. Fry rolls, a few at a time, for 3 minutes or until golden – prawns should be just cooked. Remove with a slotted spoon and drain on paper towel briefly before serving. **5** Serve with sweet chilli sauce or red vinegar with ginger for dipping.

Serves 4

vegetable oil, for deep-frying
2 × 1 kg/2 lb mud crabs, cleaned and quartered
   (see Note)
extra 100 ml/3 fl oz vegetable oil
8 teaspoons BLACK PEPPER AND LEMONGRASS
   STIR-FRY PASTE (page 82)
40 ml/1¼ fl oz Chinese oyster sauce
2 tablespoons sliced green onion/scallion

Stir-fried black pepper mud crab

1 Heat vegetable oil in a deep-fryer or large wok to 180°C/350°F and fry crab quarters for about 1 minute, or until shells change colour. Remove from oil and set aside. 2 In a separate wok, heat extra oil, add spice paste and stir-fry for 1 minute over high heat to release flavours. 3 Add oyster sauce and crab pieces and toss over heat until crab is well coated. Cook for 3 minutes. Remove from heat, sprinkle with green onion and serve.

Serves 4

Note: Other varieties of crab can be used if mud crabs are not readily available. Simply adjust the cooking time according to the type and weight of crab you are using.

Black pepper beef

40 ml/1¼ fl oz Chinese Shaoxing rice wine
20 ml/¾ fl oz fish sauce
8 teaspoons BLACK PEPPER AND LEMONGRASS
   STIR-FRY PASTE (page 82)
500 g/1 lb beef fillet, cut into 2 cm/¾ in cubes
vegetable oil, for deep-frying
2 cloves garlic, finely sliced
2 red shallots, finely sliced
40 ml/1¼ fl oz Chinese oyster sauce
20 ml/¾ fl oz light soy sauce
150 g/5 oz snow pea shoots
1 tablespoon snipped garlic chives
1 teaspoon Sichuan Spice Salt (page 200)

1 Mix rice wine with fish sauce and spice paste in a bowl. Add beef and rub in marinade to coat thoroughly and until all moisture has been absorbed by the meat. Cover and leave at room temperature for 30 minutes. **2** Heat oil in a wok and deep-fry beef for 1 minute. Remove with a slotted spoon, drain on paper towel and set aside. **3** Drain oil from wok, leaving about 1 tablespoon. Fry garlic and shallot briefly until they begin to colour, then add beef with oyster and soy sauces. Cook over high heat for 1–2 minutes, tossing regularly for even cooking. Remove from wok and set aside. **4** In the same hot wok, toss snow pea shoots and garlic chives for a few seconds to wilt and pick up remaining flavours. **5** Arrange greens on serving plates and top with pepper beef. Sprinkle with Sichuan spice salt and serve.

Serves 4

Note: This beef is fabulous with Green Bean Sambal (page 45).

4 × 125 g/4 oz white fish fillets (see Note)
4 teaspoons BLACK PEPPER AND LEMONGRASS
    STIR-FRY PASTE (page 82)
150 ml/5 fl oz Fish Stock (page 201)
40 ml/1¼ fl oz sweet soy sauce/kecap manis
20 ml/¾ fl oz fish sauce
½ cup coriander/cilantro/Chinese parsley leaves
steamed rice, to serve

Steamed spiced fish

1 Lay fish fillets on a large plate with a lip that will fit into a steamer basket. Mix spice paste with stock, soy sauce and fish sauce and pour over fish. **2** Place plate in steamer basket, cover with lid and steam over boiling water for 6–8 minutes, depending on thickness and density of fish. Flesh should be opaque when cooked. **3** Remove fish from steamer. Carefully slide onto serving plates and spoon sauce over. Add coriander leaves and serve with steamed rice.

Serves 4

Note: Any of these fish is suitable – Murray cod, snapper, bream, gurnard, sea bass, perch, coral trout, warehou, blue eye, pike.

vegetable oil, for deep-frying

4 fresh beancurd/tofu squares, sliced

20 ml/¾ fl oz chilli oil

8 teaspoons BLACK PEPPER AND LEMONGRASS
STIR-FRY PASTE (page 82)

6 candlenuts, ground

400 ml/12½ fl oz White Chicken Stock (page 202)

150 ml/5 fl oz coconut milk

100 g/3½ oz sweet potato, cooked and puréed

2 chicken breasts, finely sliced

400 g/12½ oz fresh Hokkien egg noodles, blanched

150 g/5 oz bean sprouts

4 green onions/scallions, finely sliced

1 small cucumber, chopped

1 large green chilli, seeded and finely sliced

½ cup chopped Chinese celery/kun choy *or* plain celery

3 teaspoons fish sauce

¼ cup coriander/cilantro/Chinese parsley leaves

4 teaspoons Fried Shallot Slices (page 201)

1 lime, quartered

Spicy chicken noodles with beancurd

1 Heat vegetable oil in a wok and fry beancurd, a few slices at a time, over high heat, turning carefully with a mesh spoon until golden and puffed. Remove carefully and drain on paper towel. Discard oil. **2** Heat chilli oil in wok and fry spice paste and ground candlenuts over low heat until fragrant. Add stock, coconut milk and sweet potato purée and bring to the boil. The purée will thicken the sauce as it cooks. **3** Reduce heat, stir in chicken and cook for 2 minutes. Add noodles, bean sprouts, green onion, cucumber, chilli and celery and cook for 2 minutes, or until warmed through. Add fish sauce. Taste and, if necessary, adjust seasoning. **4** Ladle into deep bowls and top with fried beancurd, coriander leaves, fried shallots and lime wedges.

Serves 4

Satay Spice Paste

Typical of Malay Nonya and Indonesian cooking, this paste is used as a marinade and flavour booster for meat, poultry or seafood, which can then be threaded on satay sticks and barbecued or grilled. The flavours are redolent of the street carts whose vendors ply these delicacies throughout much of South-East Asia. As a snack, satay has universal appeal. For best results cook over glowing charcoal embers. Satay spice paste can just as easily be used in other quick-cooking applications such as stir-frying, deep-frying or pan-frying.

1 teaspoon fennel seeds
1 teaspoon cumin seeds
2 teaspoons coriander seeds
½ teaspoon black peppercorns
30 g/1 oz palm sugar/jaggery, shaved
200 ml/6½ fl oz coconut milk
2 teaspoons ground turmeric
½ teaspoon chilli powder
1 teaspoon finely chopped lime rind/zest
2 teaspoons sea salt

Satay spice paste

1 Dry-roast whole spices separately over gentle heat until fragrant. Cool, then grind to a fine powder. **2** Stir palm sugar into coconut milk over gentle heat until it has dissolved, then mix in all spices and flavourings. Keeps, refrigerated, for up to 48 hours.

Makes about 300 ml/10 fl oz

2 teaspoons finely chopped garlic

8 teaspoons SATAY SPICE PASTE (page 96)

2 teaspoons sea salt

150 g/5 oz chickpea flour/besan

1 teaspoon baking powder

125 ml/4 fl oz water

vegetable oil, for deep-frying

2 cups diced *or* chopped mixed vegetables (cauliflower,
broccoli, potato, peas, carrot, zucchini/courgette,
eggplant/aubergine)

Spicy vegetable fritters

1 To make batter, combine garlic, SATAY SPICE PASTE and salt in a food processor. Blend in flour and baking powder, then add water and mix to a smooth batter. Refrigerate for 2 hours before using. The batter should have reasonable body without being too thick. If it looks too thick, add a little water. **2** Heat vegetable oil to 180°C/350°F in a deep-fryer or large pot. **3** Add chopped vegetables to batter. Drop spoonfuls of battered vegetable, a few at a time, into hot oil and fry for 4 minutes, or until golden and crisp. Remove fritters from oil with a slotted spoon, drain on paper towel and keep warm. Repeat process until all batter has been used. Serve with a yoghurt-based dip or raita.

Serves 4

500 g/1 lb cleaned squid tubes (see Note)
4 teaspoons SATAY SPICE PASTE (page 96)
3 cloves garlic, finely chopped
1 teaspoon ground turmeric
20 ml/¾ fl oz vegetable oil
20 ml/¾ fl oz Tamarind Liquid (page 200)
2 teaspoons sweet soy sauce/kecap manis

Stir-fried turmeric squid

1 Split squid tubes in half lengthwise and cut into strips 2.5 cm/1 in wide. Carefully score inner flesh diagonally. **2** Mix SATAY SPICE PASTE with garlic and turmeric and marinate squid in this for 30 minutes. **3** Heat oil in a wok or cast-iron pan and fry squid over high heat for 1 minute, or until it begins to curl. **4** Add tamarind liquid and sweet soy sauce and toss over heat to combine. Cook for another minute and remove from heat. Serve immediately as a snack or as part of a selection of dishes.

Serves 4

Note: If you clean your own squid, don't discard the tentacles – add them to the marinade.

Vegetable curry puffs

2 large potatoes, peeled and diced
2 sweet potatoes, peeled and diced
40 ml/1¼ fl oz vegetable oil
1 medium-size brown onion, finely diced
3 cloves garlic, minced
2 teaspoons minced ginger
8 teaspoons SATAY SPICE PASTE (page 96)
¼ cup peas
½ teaspoon sea salt
½ teaspoon freshly ground black pepper
extra vegetable oil, for deep-frying
Pastry
500 g/1 lb plain/all-purpose flour
1 teaspoon sea salt
50 g/1½ oz lard
100 g/3½ oz unsalted butter
200 ml/6½ fl oz water

1 To make the pastry, mix flour and salt, then, using your hands, work lard and butter into flour until mixture resembles dry crumbs. Add water and continue to mix until dough forms. Wrap in plastic film and set aside for 1 hour. **2** Cook potato and sweet potato in lightly salted boiling water for a few minutes until softened. Remove from heat, drain and refresh in cold water to stop cooking process. Drain again and set aside until ready to use. **3** Heat oil in a frying pan and sauté onion, garlic and ginger until starting to colour. Stir in SATAY SPICE PASTE and cook for 2 minutes. Stir in potato, sweet potato and peas. Simmer gently for 2 minutes. Remove from heat and season to taste. Allow mixture to cool thoroughly before assembling pastries. **4** Roll pastry to a thickness of about 5 mm/¼ in. Cut into 8 cm/3 in circles. Put 1 tablespoon vegetable mixture into centre of each circle and fold pastry over to make a half-circle. Press edges and crimp together to secure. **5** Heat oil to 180°C/350°F in a deep-fryer or large pot. Fry a few curry puffs at a time (to maintain oil temperature) for 5 minutes or until golden. Drain on paper towel. Continue until all pastries have been cooked. Serve hot with a yoghurt-based dipping sauce or relish.

Makes 20

400 ml/12½ fl oz coconut milk
8 teaspoons SATAY SPICE PASTE (page 96)
2 kaffir lime leaves
1 red birds-eye chilli, split lengthwise
20 ml/¾ fl oz Tamarind Liquid (page 200)
20 ml/¾ fl oz fish sauce
8 hard-boiled duck eggs (see Note)
½ cup coriander/cilantro/Chinese parsley leaves
2 tablespoons Fried Shallot Slices (page 201)

Fragrant duck eggs

1 Bring coconut milk to boiling point and stir in SATAY SPICE PASTE, lime leaves and chilli. Simmer gently for 5 minutes until sauce thickens. **2** Reduce heat to a low simmer and add tamarind liquid, fish sauce and duck eggs. Simmer gently for 6–8 minutes until eggs are heated through and well coated with sauce. **3** Spoon eggs and sauce into a bowl and sprinkle with coriander leaves and fried shallot slices. Serve with crisp roti or naan bread, parathas or pappadams.

Serves 4

Note: Chicken eggs can be substituted for the duck eggs. This dish can also be served as part of a large communal feast.

Satay prawns with green papaya salad

24 green king prawns/shrimp
8 teaspoons SATAY SPICE PASTE (page 96)
Green papaya salad
30 ml/1 fl oz strained lime juice
2 teaspoons Tamarind Liquid (page 200)
20 ml/¾ fl oz Sugar Syrup (page 201) *or*
  3 teaspoons caster sugar
20 ml/¾ fl oz fish sauce
250 g/8 oz green papaya, finely shredded
1 tablespoon dried shrimps, ground
6 cherry tomatoes, quartered
1 tablespoon red shallot slices
2 red birds-eye *or* serrano chillies, finely sliced
1 tablespoon shredded basil leaves
2 tablespoons raw peanuts, lightly roasted and
  roughly chopped

1 Soak 12 wooden skewers in water for 1 hour (to prevent them burning during cooking). Peel and devein prawns, leaving their tails intact, and marinate in SATAY SPICE PASTE for 30 minutes. **2** Thread 2 prawns onto each satay stick. **3** To make papaya salad, mix lime juice, tamarind liquid, sugar syrup and fish sauce together. Combine remaining ingredients in a bowl, keeping aside 2 teaspoons chopped peanuts, and toss with dressing. **4** Cook prawns over charcoal on a barbecue or on or under a grill for about 3–4 minutes only, or until just cooked. Remove skewers and serve prawns on papaya salad, sprinkled with remaining nuts.
Serves 4

400 g/12½ oz chicken breasts, cut into thin
    strips 2.5 cm/1 in long
8 teaspoons SATAY SPICE PASTE (page 96)
4 tablespoons Peanut Chilli Sauce (page 7)

Satay chicken with peanut chilli sauce

1 Soak wooden skewers in water for 1 hour (to prevent them burning during cooking). Marinate chicken in SATAY SPICE PASTE for 30 minutes to 1 hour. **2** Thread 3 pieces of chicken onto each skewer, keeping pieces close together to maintain moisture during cooking. Cook on a hot cast-iron grill pan or barbecue or under a grill for 5–6 minutes, turning for even cooking. The meat will become firm when cooked, but cooking time will depend on the thickness of the pieces. **3** Meanwhile, heat peanut chilli sauce in a saucepan. **4** Serve satay chicken with sauce.

Serves 4

40 ml/1¼ fl oz vegetable oil
8 red shallots
8 teaspoons SATAY SPICE PASTE (page 96)
4 teaspoons hot curry powder
2 teaspoons CHILLI JAM (page 6)
1 kg/2 lb beef rump *or* topside, cut into 2 cm/¾ in cubes
2 ripe tomatoes, peeled and chopped
1 stalk lemongrass, cut in half
400 ml/12½ fl oz thick plain yoghurt
200 ml/6½ fl oz pouring cream
20 ml/¾ fl oz fish sauce
2 teaspoons strained lime juice
steamed basmati rice, to serve

Spiced beef korma

1 Preheat oven to low (150°C/300°F). Heat oil in a large ovenproof wok or pot and fry shallots with SATAY SPICE PASTE, curry powder and CHILLI JAM, stirring often to prevent burning, for 2–3 minutes or until fragrant. **2** Add beef and stir to coat thoroughly with spice paste. Cook for 5 minutes to brown meat. **3** Add tomato, lemongrass, yoghurt and cream and bring to simmering point over gentle heat. **4** Cover pot with a lid and cook in oven for 25 minutes. Check pot – if korma appears dry, add a little water to keep it moist. Return pot to oven for 20 minutes, or until sauce has been completely absorbed by meat. **5** Remove pot from oven. Discard lemongrass stalks and season korma with fish sauce and lime juice. The curry should have a characteristic rich, oily finish. Serve with steamed basmati rice.

Serves 4

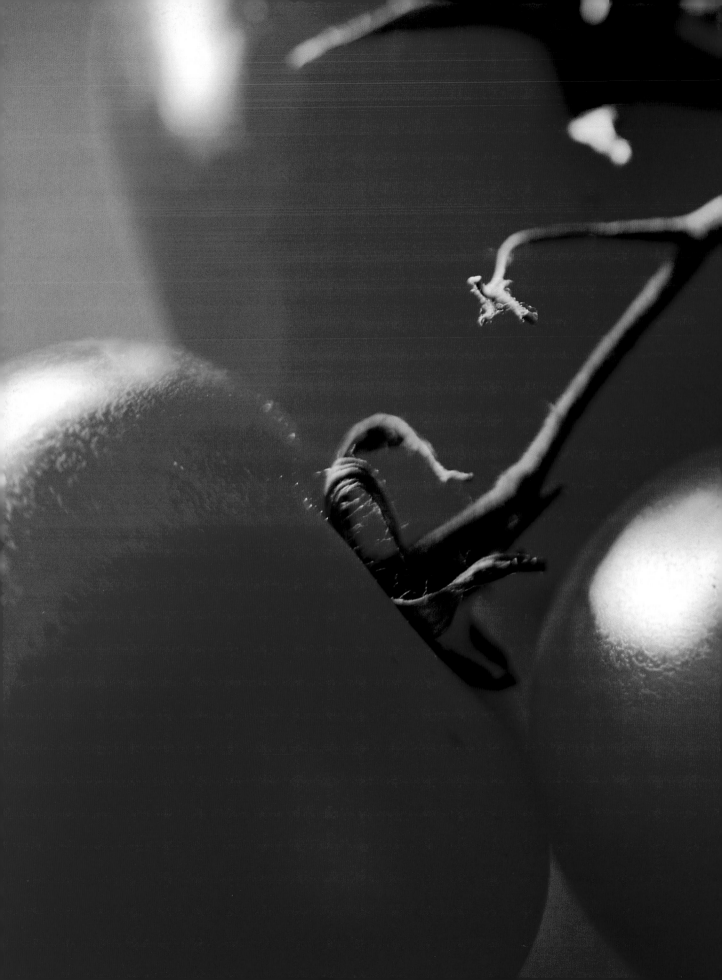

Spiced Tomato Chilli Pickle

This relish is of south Indian origin and is known on the subcontinent as tomato kasaundi. It is traditionally served as a condiment with breads and fish dishes, but you will find its flavour extremely versatile and easily adaptable to a variety of uses, not restricted to Indian-style preparations. It has a characteristic sweet–sour, spicy flavour with the chilli component being very mild on the palate, much like pepper. Serve it simply as a dipping sauce with vegetable antipasto or fried savoury pastries, or stir it into lentils or through noodles or pasta.

Spiced tomato chilli pickle

4 teaspoons brown mustard seeds
125 ml/4 fl oz cider vinegar
8 teaspoons cumin seeds
125 ml/4 fl oz vegetable oil
pinch of freshly ground cloves
2 teaspoons ground turmeric
8 teaspoons finely chopped ginger
10 cloves garlic
10 small red birds-eye chillies
2 kg/4½ lb ripe tomatoes, peeled and quartered
75 g/2½ oz palm sugar/jaggery, shaved
60 ml/2 fl oz fish sauce

1 Cook mustard seeds in vinegar over moderate heat for 10 minutes, then set aside for 2 hours. **2** Dry-roast cumin seeds over gentle heat until fragrant. Cool, then grind to a fine powder. **3** Heat oil in a heavy-based pan and fry ground cumin, cloves and turmeric gently until fragrant. Remove from heat. **4** Process mustard-seed mixture, ginger, garlic and chillies in an electric blender until smooth and add to oil and spices. Add tomato and cook over low heat, stirring frequently, for 1 hour, or until tomato has broken down and sauce is quite smooth. **5** Add palm sugar and fish sauce and cook for a further 30 minutes. Taste and, if necessary, adjust seasoning. **6** Spoon into sterilised jars, cover with a film of oil and seal when cool. Keeps, refrigerated, for 1 month.

Makes about 500 ml/16 fl oz

12 tomatoes, cut in half lengthwise
50 g/1½ oz ghee
2 medium-size brown onions, chopped
6 cloves garlic, finely chopped
2 teaspoons chopped ginger
2 red birds-eye *or* serrano chillies, finely chopped
seeds from 8 green cardamom pods, ground
1 teaspoon Garam Masala (page 200)
8 teaspoons SPICED TOMATO CHILLI PICKLE (page 108)
500 ml/16 fl oz Brown Chicken Stock (page 202)
1 teaspoon sea salt
1 teaspoon freshly ground black pepper

Tomato-cardamom sauce

1 Preheat oven to moderately hot (200°C/400°F) and roast tomatoes on a baking tray for 25 minutes. Cool. Pass through a conical sieve or food mill, pressing to extract as much juice and pulp as possible. Discard seeds and skin. **2** Melt ghee in a wide, heavy-based saucepan and fry onion, garlic, ginger and chilli until fragrant and softened. Add cardamom and garam masala and fry, stirring, for a few minutes, or until fragrant. **3** Add reserved tomato pulp and SPICED TOMATO CHILLI PICKLE and cook over high heat until bubbling. Lower heat and simmer for 10 minutes, or until slightly reduced. **4** Add stock and continue to simmer for 20 minutes. Season with salt and pepper. Cool, skimming surface when necessary. Reheat gently as required and serve with grilled fish or roasted poultry or meat.

Makes about 600 ml/20 fl oz

vegetable oil, for deep-frying

8 asparagus spears, trimmed to 5 cm/2 in lengths

8 lengthwise slices zucchini/courgette

1 green capsicum/bell pepper, cut into eighths lengthwise
   and seeded

4 green onions/scallions, cut into 5 cm/2 in lengths

plain/all-purpose flour

Tempura Batter (page 201)

8 basil leaves

8 large mint leaves

4 sprigs of flat-leaf parsley

4 tablespoons SPICED TOMATO CHILLI PICKLE (page 108)

Green vegetable tempura with spiced tomato chilli pickle

1 Heat oil in a deep-fryer or large pot to 180°C/350°F. Dust vegetables and herbs with flour, then dip into tempura batter. **2** Deep-fry vegetables and herbs in hot oil, a few pieces at a time, for 1 minute. Remove with a slotted spoon and drain on paper towel. **3** Pile vegetable tempura on a large plate and serve with SPICED TOMATO CHILLI PICKLE as a condiment.

Serves 4

Spaghetti with crabmeat, pimiento and spiced tomato chilli pickle

250 g/8 oz spaghetti
50 ml/1½ fl oz extra-virgin olive oil
4 teaspoons Saffron Butter (page 200)
1 small red/Spanish onion, finely chopped
6 cloves garlic, finely chopped
2 small red birds-eye *or* serrano chillies, finely chopped
2 tomatoes, peeled, seeded and finely chopped
8 teaspoons SPICED TOMATO CHILLI PICKLE (page 108)
75 g/2½ oz roasted strips pimiento/Spanish piquillo
   pepper
500 g/1 lb cooked crabmeat (blue swimmer, spanner
   or mud crab)
½ cup shaved fennel bulb
1 teaspoon sea salt
1 teaspoon freshly ground black pepper
¼ cup torn basil leaves

1 Cook spaghetti in a large pot of lightly salted boiling water. **2** Meanwhile, heat oil and saffron butter in a heavy-based frying pan. Add onion, garlic and chilli and cook gently for 1 minute until fragrant, but not coloured. **3** Add tomato, SPICED TOMATO CHILLI PICKLE and pimiento strips and cook until simmering. **4** Add crabmeat and fennel and toss over heat to combine. Season with salt and pepper. **5** Drain pasta and toss with a little extra oil. Add crab sauce and basil and toss to coat pasta. Ladle pasta into bowls to serve. *Serves 4*

4 × 125 g/4 oz red salmon fillets, with skin

extra-virgin olive oil

½ teaspoon sea salt

½ teaspoon freshly ground black pepper

Spiced red capsicum sauce

3 red capsicums/bell peppers

40 ml/1¼ fl oz olive oil

1 large brown onion, diced

3 cloves garlic, finely diced

2 small red birds-eye *or* serrano chillies, chopped

sea salt, to taste

freshly ground black pepper, to taste

8 teaspoons SPICED TOMATO CHILLI PICKLE (page 108)

100 ml/3½ fl oz pouring cream

Seared salmon with spiced red capsicum sauce

1 To make sauce, preheat oven to moderately hot (200°C/400°F). Rub capsicums with a little oil and roast on a baking tray for 30 minutes, or until capsicums are blistered and blackened on the surface. Remove from heat and cool slightly. Remove skins, stalk ends and seeds. **2** Heat remaining oil in a frying pan and cook onion, garlic and chilli until soft and golden. Remove from heat. **3** Process roasted capsicums with onion mixture in an electric blender or food processor until smooth. Pass through a conical sieve or food mill, pressing as hard as possible to extract as much juice and pulp as possible. Discard solids and season to taste. Reheat sauce to simmering point in a pan with SPICED TOMATO CHILLI PICKLE and cream. **4** To cook fish, preheat oven to moderate (180°C/350°F). Heat an ovenproof frying pan, add a little oil and add salmon fillets, skin-side down. Sprinkle with salt and pepper and fry over moderately high heat for 2 minutes, or until juices are sealed in and skin is crisp. Place pan in oven for 4 minutes. Remove fish from oven and carefully slide fillets onto warmed plates. Serve with spiced red capsicum sauce.

Serves 4

Saffron scallops with spiced tomato sauce

2 bunches spinach, stems removed

4 tablespoons SPICED TOMATO CHILLI PICKLE (page 108)

8 teaspoons Saffron Butter (page 200)

16 fresh, plump sea scallops

¼ cup coriander/cilantro/Chinese parsley leaves

2 tablespoons shredded mint leaves

2 ripe medium-size tomatoes, peeled, seeded and diced

½ teaspoon sea salt

½ teaspoon freshly ground black pepper

30 g/1 oz unsalted butter

8 spearmint leaves, shredded

1 Wash spinach thoroughly. Blanch in boiling water for 30 seconds and refresh immediately in iced water. When cold, squeeze out water. **2** Bring SPICED TOMATO CHILLI PICKLE to a simmer in a saucepan over moderate heat. Stir in saffron butter and scallops and cook, stirring regularly, over gentle heat for 3 minutes. Remove from heat and stir in coriander, mint and tomato and season with salt and pepper. **3** Melt butter in a saucepan, add spinach and reheat gently, stirring. Season to taste. Divide spinach between 4 plates, top with spiced scallops, spoon sauce around and garnish with shredded spearmint leaves. Serve immediately.

Serves 4

Note: If your scallops are particularly large, this recipe will serve 8 people as a 'taster'. Serve 1 scallop per person, as in the photograph opposite.

Salt-baked barramundi with spiced tomato chilli sauce

2 kg/4 lb rock salt

1 whole 2 kg/4½ lb wild *or* sea-farmed barramundi, cleaned and scaled (see Note)

4 quarters PRESERVED LEMON (page 124)

1 bunch dill

½ teaspoon sea salt

1 teaspoon freshly ground black pepper

4 tablespoons SPICED TOMATO CHILLI PICKLE (page 108)

50 g/1½ oz unsalted butter

2 teaspoons lemon juice

1 Preheat oven to hot (220°C/450°F). Lay half the rock salt in the base of a roasting tray large enough to hold the fish. **2** Chop PRESERVED LEMON and place inside fish cavity with dill. Season fish cavity with sea salt and pepper. **3** Lay fish on salt base and cover with remaining rock salt, leaving tail out. Cover tail with foil. Bake for 15 minutes (less for smaller fish), then test with a skewer to see if the fish is warm right through. It may require a further 5 minutes or so, but be careful not to overcook it or fish will dry out. **4** Remove fish from heat and rest for 5 minutes. Scrape off rock salt and skin before fish cools. **5** Heat SPICED TOMATO CHILLI PICKLE to simmering point with butter and lemon juice. Carefully lift fish out of tray and discard lemon filling. Portion fish evenly and serve with sauce.

Serves 8

Note: Fish such as halibut, Chilean sea bass or snapper can be substituted for barramundi.

4 × 150 g/5 oz yellowfin tuna steaks (see Note)

20 ml/¾ fl oz olive oil

1 teaspoon freshly ground black pepper

½ teaspoon cayenne pepper

½ teaspoon sea salt

Tomato and pepper salsa

4 ripe tomatoes, peeled, seeded and finely diced

2 red capsicums/bell peppers, roasted and finely diced

2 yellow capsicums/bell peppers, roasted and finely diced

1 small red onion, finely diced

4 teaspoons SPICED TOMATO CHILLI PICKLE (page 108)

½ cup flat-leaf parsley leaves, shredded

2 tablespoons small capers, washed

125 ml/4 fl oz extra-virgin olive oil

Grilled tuna steaks with tomato and pepper salsa

1 To make the salsa, combine all ingredients. Set aside until ready to serve. **2** Brush each tuna steak with oil and season with pepper and cayenne. Char-grill, grill or barbecue steaks on medium–high heat for 3 minutes. Turn steaks and cook for an extra minute, leaving them quite rare in the centre to retain maximum moisture. Remove from heat and sprinkle with sea salt. **3** Serve with tomato and pepper salsa and a salad of green leaves or rocket/arugula.

Serves 4

Note: Swordfish, marlin, dolphin fish or Chilean sea bass can be substituted for tuna.

Baked goat's cheese and pimiento tarts with spiced tomato chilli pickle

4 teaspoons Caramelised Onion (page 201)

4 × 7.5 cm/3 in shortcrust tart shells, baked blind

150 g/5 oz fresh goat's cheese/chèvre, slightly crumbled

1 tablespoon roasted strips pimiento/Spanish piquillo pepper, finely sliced

1 egg

1 tablespoon crème fraîche

½ teaspoon sea salt

¼ teaspoon freshly ground black pepper

1 tablespoon flat-leaf parsley, shredded

3 tablespoons SPICED TOMATO CHILLI PICKLE (page 108)

1 Preheat oven to moderate (180°C/350°F). **2** Spread 1 teaspoon caramelised onion on base of each tart shell. Pile goat's cheese on top and arrange some pimiento strips around the cheese. **3** Mix egg and crème fraîche and season with salt and pepper. Spoon into tart shells until full. **4** Bake tarts for 10 minutes, or until just set. (Cooking time will vary if different-sized tart shells are used.) Remove from oven and sprinkle with parsley. Serve with warmed SPICED TOMATO CHILLI PICKLE.

Makes 4

Lamb's brain fritters with tomato-cardamom sauce

4 sets lamb's brains
1 tablespoon plain/all-purpose flour
2 eggs, beaten
sea salt
freshly ground white pepper
2 tablespoons fine breadcrumbs
125 ml/4 fl oz Tomato-cardamom Sauce (page 109)
2 tablespoons diced tomato
2 tablespoons shredded flat-leaf parsley
vegetable oil, for deep-frying
60 g/2 oz rocket/arugula leaves

1 Poach lamb's brains in simmering water for 2 minutes. Remove from heat and plunge into ice-cold water to stop cooking. **2** Separate lobes and peel brains, discarding membrane. Slice each lobe in half lengthwise. Dust pieces in flour, then dip in beaten egg and coat with seasoned breadcrumbs. Rest on paper towel until ready to cook. **3** Heat tomato-cardamom sauce gently. Stir in tomato and parsley. **4** Heat oil in a deep-fryer or large pot to 180°C/350°F and fry brains, a few pieces at a time (to maintain oil temperature), for 2 minutes. Remove with a slotted spoon and drain on paper towel. **5** Sit rocket leaves on plates and arrange brain fritters on top. Spoon tomato-cardamom sauce over and serve.

Serves 4

12 × 11 cm/4½ in square spring roll wrappers

1 egg white

vegetable oil, for deep-frying

4 tablespoons SPICED TOMATO CHILLI PICKLE (page 108)

Beef stuffing

20 ml/¾ fl oz vegetable oil

1 medium-size brown onion, finely chopped

3 cloves garlic, finely chopped

1 tablespoon mild curry powder

2 teaspoons CHILLI JAM (page 6)

185 g/6 oz minced beef

125 g/4 oz potatoes, boiled and finely diced

2 tablespoons coriander/cilantro/Chinese parsley leaves

½ teaspoon sea salt

½ teaspoon freshly ground black pepper

Beef and potato pastries with spiced tomato chilli pickle

1 To make beef stuffing, heat oil and fry onion and garlic until lightly coloured. Add curry powder and fry for about 2 minutes. Stir in CHILLI JAM and minced beef and cook over moderate heat for 5 minutes, or until meat is just cooked through. Remove from heat and cool. Mix potato and coriander into cooled meat mixture and season. Allow stuffing to cool completely before assembling pastries. **2** Lay a spring roll wrapper on a board and place some beef stuffing in centre. Fold pastry over and fold in edges to seal into a log shape. Brush open edge with egg white and roll over to seal. **3** Heat oil in a deep-fryer or large pot to 180°C/350°F and deep-fry the pastries, a few at a time (to maintain oil temperature), for 2 minutes or until golden. Remove with a slotted spoon and drain on paper towel. **4** Serve with SPICED TOMATO CHILLI PICKLE as a dipping sauce.

Makes 12

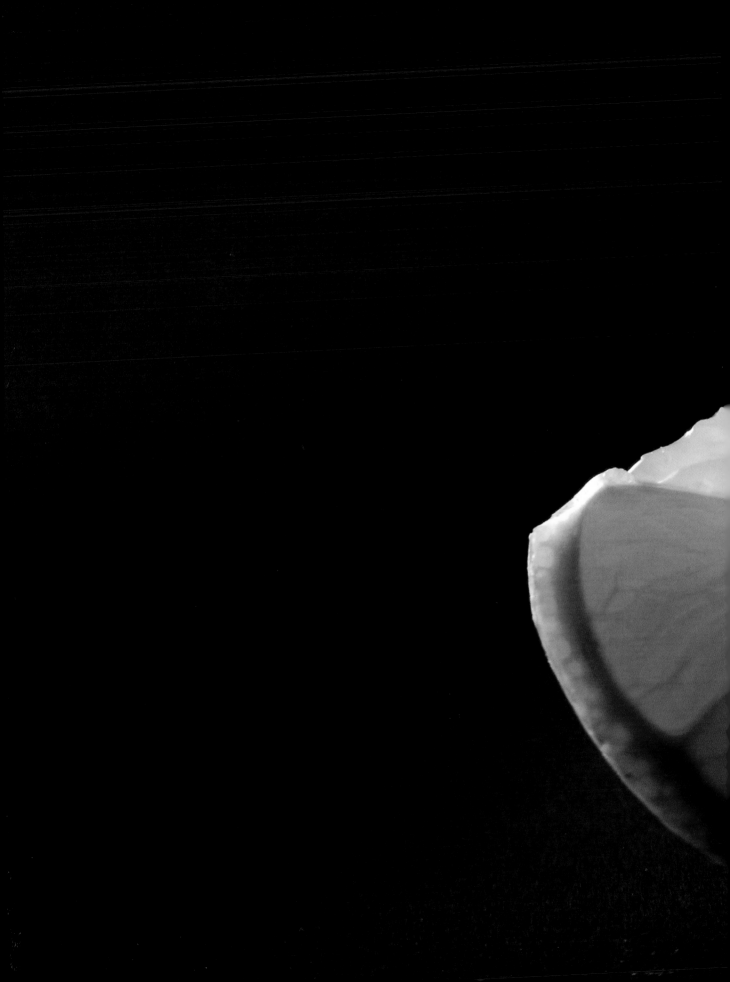

Preserved Lemons

Lemons are an essential element in many cooking processes. A natural agent of change, their acidity brings balance and harmony to food. Lemons enhance flavours and, when preserved, give them an incomparable complexity. Fresh lemon rind/zest or its juice is no substitute for the smooth mellow character of a preserved lemon. Often used in conjunction with aromatic spices and herbs, preserved lemons provide a foil to the richness of meat and the oiliness of fish and olives, while at the same time transforming an 'acceptable' dish into a taste sensation.

8 ripe lemons
250 g/8 oz fine table salt
lemon juice, to cover

Preserved lemons

1 Wash lemons thoroughly, scrubbing skins if necessary. Cut into quarters lengthwise to within 1 cm/½ in of base. Pack each piece with salt and reshape fruit by pressing back together. 2 Put lemons into a sterilised 2 litre/2 quart preserving jar and sprinkle with a little extra salt. Cover with lemon juice. Seal and store for 6 weeks in a cool place away from direct light. 3 When lemons are ready to use, remove from jar as needed and rinse with water before proceeding. Discard flesh and use only the rind/zest in any of the preparations given here. If stored in a cool place away from light, PRESERVED LEMONS will keep for 6 months.

2 ripe avocados, chopped
1 clove garlic, finely chopped
1 teaspoon CHILLI JAM (page 6)
½ teaspoon sea salt
¼ teaspoon freshly ground black pepper
2 teaspoons lemon juice
8 cherry tomatoes, quartered
rind/zest of 1 PRESERVED LEMON (page 124),
    finely diced
2 tablespoons chopped coriander/cilantro/
    Chinese parsley leaves

Preserved lemon guacamole

1 In a food processor, blend avocado with garlic, CHILLI JAM, salt, pepper and lemon juice until smooth.

2 Spoon into a bowl and stir through the tomato, PRESERVED LEMON rind and coriander. Serve as a dip with crusty bread, wafers or corn chips or as an accompaniment to grilled fish or barbecued poultry.

Serves 4

500 g/1 lb kalamata olives
2 teaspoons cumin seeds, roasted
rind/zest of 1 PRESERVED LEMON (page 124),
    cut into strips
2 small red birds-eye *or* serrano chillies, finely sliced
2 cloves garlic
2 sprigs of thyme *or* flat-leaf parsley, shredded
1 teaspoon black peppercorns
250 ml/8 fl oz extra-virgin olive oil

Spiced black olives with preserved lemon

1 Place all ingredients in a clean jar and cover with oil. **2** Remove from oil as required and serve with drinks or use to flavour pasta or a fetta cheese salad.

Chermoula with preserved lemon

1 teaspoon cumin seeds

10 red shallots, finely sliced

4 large cloves garlic, finely chopped

¼ cup flat-leaf parsley, finely chopped

½ cup coriander/cilantro/Chinese parsley leaves, finely chopped

½ cup spearmint leaves, finely chopped

2 red birds-eye chillies, finely chopped

½ teaspoon freshly ground black pepper

rind/zest of ½ PRESERVED LEMON (page 124), diced

200 ml/6½ fl oz extra-virgin olive oil

1 Mix all ingredients thoroughly. **2** Spoon into a jar and cover with a film of oil. Keeps, refrigerated, for up to 3 days. Use when cooking fish or chicken, or toss with boiled potatoes.

Makes about 350 ml/11 fl oz

200 g/6½ oz fresh tuna (canned tuna can be substituted)
½ teaspoon freshly ground black pepper
200 ml/6½ fl oz extra-virgin olive oil
sea salt
250 g/8 oz spaghetti
½ fennel bulb, finely shaved
1 tablespoon finely chopped garlic
40 ml/1¼ fl oz lemon juice
3 tablespoons shredded flat-leaf parsley
1 tablespoon small capers, washed
1 tablespoon finely sliced *or* chopped rind/zest of
   PRESERVED LEMON (page 124)

Spaghetti with tuna, preserved lemon, capers and fennel

1 Sprinkle tuna lightly with pepper. Heat a little of the oil in a frying pan and sear tuna on both sides over high heat for 2 minutes. Remove from heat and allow to cool briefly, then slice finely. **2** Heat a large pot of water to boiling point, add a pinch of salt and cook spaghetti until al dente. Drain immediately. **3** Meanwhile, combine remaining oil, tuna, fennel, garlic, lemon juice, parsley, capers and PRESERVED LEMON rind in a large bowl. Season to taste with salt and pepper. **4** Toss pasta through tuna mixture and serve immediately.

Serves 4

150 ml/5 fl oz Chermoula with Preserved Lemon
   (page 128)
4 × 125 g/4 oz salmon fillets, taken from thickest part
   of fish (see Note)
2 bunches spinach, stalks removed
50 g/1½ oz unsalted butter
½ teaspoon sea salt
½ teaspoon freshly ground black pepper
pinch of freshly grated nutmeg
4 teaspoons extra-virgin olive oil

Baked salmon with preserved lemon chermoula

1 Prepare 4 sheets of baking paper and 4 sheets of foil, each 20 cm/8 in square. On each piece of baking paper, spread 4 teaspoons chermoula and lay a salmon fillet on top. Spread another 4 teaspoons chermoula on top of each fillet. Fold paper over to make secure packages, then wrap each in foil. Allow salmon to marinate for 30 minutes at room temperature before cooking. Preheat oven to moderately hot (200°C/400°F). **2** Wash spinach leaves thoroughly, blanch in boiling water for 30 seconds and refresh immediately in iced water to stop cooking process and retain green colour. Squeeze out excess water and set aside until ready to use. **3** Bake salmon parcels on a baking tray for 8–10 minutes, depending on thickness of fillets. The fish should have a rosy blush in the middle to retain maximum moisture. **4** While fish is baking, heat a frying pan and melt butter over low heat. Add spinach, salt, pepper and nutmeg. Stir continually over medium heat for about 4 minutes, or until spinach has softened and is warmed through. **5** When fish is cooked, remove parcels from oven and unwrap. Spoon spinach onto 4 plates and slide fish on top. Pour over any juices from the packets and drizzle each serving with 1 teaspoon olive oil.

Serves 4

Note: For variety, substitute ocean trout, freshwater salmon, Arctic char, halibut or Chilean sea bass for the salmon.

Rice pilaf with raisins, pine nuts, preserved lemon and herbs

75 g/2½ oz ghee

1 medium-size onion, finely chopped

2 cloves garlic, finely chopped

1 stick of cinnamon

200 g/6½ oz basmati rice

40 g/1¼ oz pine nuts, lightly roasted

40 g/1¼ oz raisins

500 ml/16 fl oz water

2 teaspoons chopped chervil

1 teaspoon chopped mint leaves

2 teaspoons chopped flat-leaf parsley

1 teaspoon chopped coriander/cilantro/Chinese parsley leaves

4 teaspoons diced rind/zest of PRESERVED LEMON (page 124)

1 teaspoon sea salt

1 teaspoon freshly ground black pepper

1 Heat ghee in a large pan and cook onion and garlic over moderate heat for about 3 minutes, or until softened. **2** Add cinnamon stick and rice and stir to coat with onion mixture. Add pine nuts, raisins and water. **3** Cover pan with a lid, reduce heat to low and simmer for 15–20 minutes, or until liquid has been absorbed and rice is cooked. Remove cinnamon stick and discard. **4** Remove pan from heat and stir in chopped herbs and PRESERVED LEMON rind. Season with salt and pepper. Serve with fried fish, steamed chicken, grilled lamb or roasted beef.

Serves 4

250 g/8 oz tagliatelle *or* other pasta
125 g/4 oz fetta cheese, slightly crumbled (see Note)
200 g/6½ oz cherry tomatoes, halved and lightly roasted
rind/zest of 1 PRESERVED LEMON (page 124), diced
1 tablespoon shredded flat-leaf parsley
12 basil leaves, shredded
100 ml/3½ fl oz extra-virgin olive oil
8 cloves garlic, roasted
1 teaspoon sea salt
1 teaspoon freshly ground black pepper
4 teaspoons freshly grated parmesan cheese

Fetta, preserved lemon and tomato pasta

1 Cook pasta in salted boiling water until al dente. Drain. **2** Combine remaining ingredients, except parmesan, in a bowl, add hot pasta and toss to mix well. Sprinkle with parmesan and serve immediately.

Serves 4

Note: Ricotta or fresh goat's cheese can be used in place of fetta cheese.

Saffron tomato soup with grilled rouget fillet and prawns

12 ripe tomatoes
125 ml/4 fl oz extra-virgin olive oil
1 small brown onion, finely chopped
4 cloves garlic, finely chopped
2 teaspoons diced fennel bulb
1 red birds-eye chilli, finely chopped
1 small leek, finely diced
1 tablespoon diced carrot
½ teaspoon fennel seeds, roasted and ground
1 litre/32 fl oz Prawn/Shrimp Stock (page 202) *or*
 Fish Stock (page 201)
½ teaspoon saffron threads
½ teaspoon sea salt
½ teaspoon freshly ground black pepper
4 rouget/red mullet/barbounia fillets
8 green prawns/shrimp, shelled and butterflied open
Preserved lemon gremolata
2 teaspoons finely chopped rind/zest of PRESERVED
 LEMON (page 124)
1 clove garlic, finely chopped
2 teaspoons chopped flat-leaf parsley

1 Preheat oven to hot (220°C/450°F). Cut tomatoes in half lengthwise, place in a single layer on a baking tray and drizzle over 50 ml/1½ fl oz of the oil. Roast for about 30 minutes, or until soft and caramelised. **2** Heat remaining oil in a pot over gentle heat and cook onion, garlic, fennel, chilli, leek, carrot and fennel seeds until softened and slightly coloured. **3** Add stock, roasted tomatoes and their juices and bring to the boil. Simmer gently for 20 minutes. Pass through a fine mesh sieve, pressing firmly to extract all juices. Discard solids. **4** Reheat broth to boiling point, add saffron and season with sea salt and pepper. **5** Make preserved lemon gremolata by mixing all ingredients together in a bowl. **6** Place fish fillets and prawns on a lightly oiled baking tray. Season lightly with salt and pepper and grill for 2–3 minutes, or until just cooked. **7** Ladle broth into serving bowls and add a fish fillet and 2 prawns per bowl. Sprinkle with gremolata and serve immediately.

Serves 4

Grilled swordfish with eggplant,
tomato, preserved lemon and olives

1 × 300g/9½ oz eggplant/aubergine
300 ml/10 fl oz extra-virgin olive oil
30 ml/1 fl oz aged (8- *or* 12-year-old) balsamic vinegar
1 teaspoon sea salt
1 teaspoon freshly ground black pepper
4 oven-dried tomatoes, cut into thin strips
8 kalamata olives, pitted and sliced
2 tablespoons chervil leaves
2 tablespoons finely sliced rind/zest of PRESERVED LEMON
   (page 124)
4 × 125 g/4 oz swordfish fillets (see Note)

1 Peel eggplant and cut into thin strips lengthwise. Heat half the oil in a frying pan and fry eggplant for about 15 minutes, or until slightly coloured and soft. Remove from heat and set aside. 2 Whisk vinegar in a bowl with salt, pepper and 80 ml/2½ fl oz of the remaining oil until emulsified. 3 In another bowl, combine fried eggplant, tomato strips, olives, chervil and PRESERVED LEMON rind. 4 Heat remaining oil in a frying pan over moderate heat and cook swordfish fillets for 2–4 minutes, depending on thickness, until cooked halfway through. Flip fillets over and cook other side. Remove carefully from pan. 5 Arrange vegetable salad on 4 plates and spoon vinaigrette over. Sit fish on top and serve.

Serves 4

Note: Tuna, kingfish, marlin, turbot, monkfish or mackerel can be substituted for the swordfish.

Chicken cous cous salad with lemon

200 g/6½ oz cous cous (see Note)
400 ml/12½ fl oz White Chicken Stock (page 202)
  or water
2 tablespoons unsalted butter
125 g/4 oz green beans, sliced diagonally
2 cooked chicken breasts, shredded
2 tablespoons diced rind/zest of PRESERVED LEMON
  (page 124)
12 cherry tomatoes, halved
8 green olives, pitted and sliced
¼ cup shredded flat-leaf parsley
¼ cup mint leaves
1 small red/Spanish onion, finely chopped
Vinaigrette
50 ml/1½ fl oz lemon juice
2 teaspoons pomegranate molasses
2 cloves garlic, finely chopped
175 ml/5½ fl oz extra-virgin olive oil
1 teaspoon sea salt
1 teaspoon freshly ground black pepper

1 Place cous cous in a bowl. Bring stock to the boil and pour over cous cous. Stir in butter and leave to stand, stirring occasionally, for 15 minutes, or until liquid has been absorbed. Cool. **2** Blanch beans and refresh in cold water. **3** Make vinaigrette by whisking all ingredients together. **4** In a large bowl, combine cous cous, beans, chicken, PRESERVED LEMON rind, tomato, olives, herbs and onion. Stir in vinaigrette and serve. *Serves 4*

Note: Cracked wheat/burghul may be substituted for the cous cous. Soak it in water for 1 hour and then blanch in boiling water for 30 seconds. Drain and allow to cool before using.

4 lamb shanks
60 ml/2 fl oz olive oil
3 teaspoons freshly ground black pepper
2 medium-size brown onions, finely chopped
6 cloves garlic, finely chopped
1 tablespoon finely chopped ginger
1 red birds-eye chilli, finely chopped
1 teaspoon ground cumin
1 teaspoon ras el hanout spice mix
½ teaspoon chilli powder *or* paprika
1.5 litres/48 fl oz Beef/Veal Stock (page 203)
8 small potatoes, thickly sliced
rind/zest of ½ PRESERVED LEMON (page 124), chopped
40 ml/1¼ fl oz lemon juice
¼ cup chervil leaves
mashed potato, steamed rice *or* cous cous, to serve

Lamb shanks with preserved lemon

1 Preheat oven to low (150°C/300°F). **2** Brush shanks with some of the oil and sprinkle with 1 teaspoon of the pepper. Brown in a large, heavy-based cast-iron casserole over moderately high heat for about 10 minutes each side. Remove meat from pot. **3** Add remaining oil and cook onion, garlic, ginger and chilli until fragrant. Stir in ground spices and remaining pepper and cook for a few minutes. **4** Pour in stock and bring to the boil. Reduce to a simmer, return shanks to pot with potato and cover with a lid. Place pot in oven and cook slowly, turning meat in the stock during cooking, for about 1½ hours. **5** Stir in PRESERVED LEMON rind and lemon juice. Cook for another 15 minutes, or until meat is very tender, almost falling off the bone. Taste and, if necessary, adjust seasoning. Add chervil as you are about to serve. Serve with mashed potato, steamed rice or cous cous.

Serves 4

Green Masala Paste

The true term for any Indian spice-mix preparation, whether it be wet or dry, is 'masala'. This is more often referred to in English-speaking countries merely as 'curry' – as if it were a generic term for a dish with a one-dimensional flavour. This particular masala paste is versatile, pungent and slightly sour and has its origins in southern India, although the use of vinegar is particular to Goa. It is used in the making of rich sauces and curries and is best suited to fish, chicken or vegetables. It can give indefinable nuances to slow-cooked preparations or simply be stirred into food towards the end of cooking to give a delicious and herbaceous burst of flavour.

Green masala paste

400 ml/12½ fl oz malt vinegar
1 tablespoon fenugreek seeds
2 teaspoons cumin seeds
3 cups chopped mint leaves
4 cups chopped coriander/cilantro/Chinese parsley leaves
25 cloves garlic, finely chopped
3 tablespoons finely chopped ginger
1 tablespoon finely chopped fresh turmeric
2 tablespoons ground turmeric
1 teaspoon freshly ground cloves
2 teaspoons freshly ground green cardamom seeds
300 ml/10 fl oz vegetable oil
50 ml/1½ fl oz sesame oil
50 ml/1½ fl oz fish sauce

1 Bring malt vinegar and fenugreek seeds to the boil in a stainless steel or enamelled saucepan. Remove from heat and set aside for 6 hours, or overnight. **2** Dry-roast cumin seeds over gentle heat until fragrant. Cool, then grind to a fine powder. **3** Process all ingredients, in small batches if necessary, to a smooth, fine paste in an electric blender or food processor. **4** Cook paste in a wide, heavy-based pan over gentle heat for 1 hour, stirring regularly and adding more oil if necessary to prevent sticking. **5** Spoon into sterilised jars, cover with a film of oil and seal when cool. Keeps, refrigerated, for 1 month.

Makes about 600 ml/20 fl oz

400 g/12½ oz potatoes, peeled and thickly sliced
2 tablespoons ghee
3 cloves garlic, finely chopped
1 teaspoon finely chopped ginger
2 small red birds-eye *or* serrano chillies, seeded and
   finely chopped
1 teaspoon ground turmeric
24 fresh curry leaves
4 teaspoons GREEN MASALA PASTE (page 142)
2 tomatoes, cut into rounds
1 tablespoon brown sugar
2 teaspoons sea salt
2 tablespoons fresh peas, blanched
2 teaspoons Garam Masala (page 200)
1 tablespoon Fried Shallot Slices (page 201)

Masala potatoes

1 Cook potatoes in boiling salted water until just cooked. Drain. **2** Melt ghee in a saucepan and fry garlic, ginger and chilli. Add turmeric, curry leaves and GREEN MASALA PASTE and fry for about 2 minutes, or until fragrant. **3** Add potato, tomato, sugar and salt. Simmer on low heat, stirring occasionally, for 10 minutes, or until tomato begins to soften. Add peas and heat through. **4** Remove from heat, sprinkle with garam masala and fried shallot slices and serve.

Serves 4

2 large eggs
1 teaspoon fish sauce
2 teaspoons ghee
1 teaspoon finely diced onion
1 teaspoon GREEN MASALA PASTE (page 142)
1 tablespoon bean sprouts
1 tablespoon snow pea sprouts
2 teaspoons coriander/cilantro/Chinese parsley leaves
1 teaspoon Fried Shallot Slices (page 201)

Individual masala omelettes

1 Whisk eggs and fish sauce in a bowl. 2 Melt ghee in an omelette pan and cook onion until starting to colour. Add GREEN MASALA PASTE and fry over moderate heat until fragrant. 3 Add egg mixture to pan, stirring with a spoon or chopstick to combine. When omelette begins to set, add bean sprouts, snow pea sprouts and coriander leaves. The omelette is ready when still soft in the centre. 4 Fold omelette in half and transfer to a warm plate. Sprinkle fried shallot slices over to serve.

Serves 1

Note: If making this dish for more than 1 person, cook an omelette at a time for best results.

Sour vegetable curry

40 ml/1¼ fl oz vegetable oil

2 small onions, sliced

3 cloves garlic, sliced

2 teaspoons finely chopped ginger

2 small green jalapeño chillies, sliced

4 teaspoons GREEN MASALA PASTE (page 142)

2 tablespoons chickpea flour/besan

100 ml/3½ fl oz coconut milk

400 ml/12½ fl oz Spiced Vegetable Stock (page 204)

100 ml/3½ fl oz Tamarind Liquid (page 200)

30 g/1 oz palm sugar/jaggery, shaved

20 ml/¾ fl oz fish sauce

1 small green mango

100 g/3½ oz sweet potato, cut into 2.5 cm/1 in dice

100 g/3½ oz small potatoes, halved

1 small carrot, cut into 2 cm/¾ in lengths

4 okra

1 fennel bulb, cut into 2 cm/¾ in thick slices

50 g/1½ oz pea eggplants/aubergines

2 tablespoons mint leaves

2 tablespoons coriander/cilantro/Chinese parsley leaves

steamed rice, to serve

1 Heat oil in a wide frying pan and fry onion, garlic, ginger and chilli until softened and beginning to colour. Stir in GREEN MASALA PASTE and fry for another 2 minutes, or until fragrant. **2** Add flour and cook, stirring constantly, over low heat until paste has thickened. Add coconut milk, stock, tamarind liquid, sugar and fish sauce and simmer for 10 minutes. **3** Peel mango and discard skin and seed. Cut into 2.5 cm/1 in dice. Add to curry with sweet potato and potato and cook for 10 minutes. **4** Add remaining vegetables and simmer for a further 15–20 minutes, or until vegetables are cooked. Taste and, if necessary, adjust seasoning. **5** Add mint and coriander leaves and serve with steamed rice.

Serves 4

Note: Water can be used instead of the Spiced Vegetable Stock.

400 g/12½ oz long pasta (spaghetti, linguine *or* tagliatelle)

75 g/2½ oz unsalted butter

2 small green jalapeño chillies, finely sliced

2 cloves garlic, finely chopped

2 teaspoons GREEN MASALA PASTE (page 142)

1 tablespoon brown sugar

2 teaspoons strained lime juice

1 green capsicum/bell pepper, seeded and finely sliced

50 g/1½ oz rocket/arugula leaves

2 tablespoons chopped coriander/cilantro/Chinese parsley
   leaves

2 tablespoon chopped Vietnamese mint/laksa leaves

1 tablespoon snipped chives *or* garlic chives

1 tablespoon chopped Thai/holy basil leaves

1 teaspoon sea salt

1 teaspoon freshly ground black pepper

Pasta tossed with herb masala

1 Cook pasta in boiling water until al dente. Drain. **2** Meanwhile, heat butter in a saucepan and fry chilli and garlic for 1 minute. Add GREEN MASALA PASTE and sugar. Cook for 5 minutes over moderate heat. **3** Add cooked pasta, lime juice, capsicum, rocket, herbs, salt and pepper. Toss thoroughly to coat pasta with the spice-and-herb mixture. Serve immediately.

Serves 4

Mussels in green masala sauce

1 kg/2 lb black mussels, shells scrubbed

2 tablespoons Saffron Butter (page 200)

1 tablespoon finely shredded mint leaves

2 tablespoons diced tomato *or* tomato cut into thin strips

blanched spinach, Chinese white cabbage/bok choy

   or roasted tomatoes, to serve

Green masala sauce

2 teaspoons ghee

1 tablespoon diced onion

½ teaspoon ground turmeric

4 teaspoons GREEN MASALA PASTE (page 142)

4 teaspoons SPICED TOMATO CHILLI PICKLE (page 108)

8 teaspoons tomato purée

150 ml/5 fl oz Fish Stock (page 201)

2 teaspoons shaved palm sugar/jaggery

20 ml/¾ fl oz fish sauce

1 To make the sauce, melt ghee in a wide, heavy-based saucepan over moderate heat and fry onion until softened. Add turmeric and fry until fragrant, then stir in GREEN MASALA PASTE and SPICED TOMATO CHILLI PICKLE. Cook for a few minutes until mixture starts to bubble, then stir in tomato purée and cook for another minute. Add stock and cook gently for 25 minutes, or until slightly thickened. Stir in sugar and fish sauce and cook for 5 minutes, stirring until sugar has dissolved. 2 Toss mussels into a separate wide, heavy-based saucepan over high heat. Cover and steam until shells open. This will take only about 1 minute. Remove open mussels (discard any that haven't opened or are broken) and plunge into iced water to stop the cooking process. Drain. When cool, remove mussels from shells. Discard shells. 3 To serve, bring sauce to the boil and add mussels, saffron butter, mint and tomato. Stir over moderate heat to work in butter. Taste and, if necessary, adjust seasoning. As soon as butter has been incorporated, remove pan from heat and serve with blanched spinach, Chinese cabbage/bok choy or roasted tomatoes.

Serves 4

500 g/1 lb green tomatoes
80 ml/2½ fl oz vegetable oil
1 medium-size brown onion, finely sliced
4 teaspoons GREEN MASALA PASTE (page 142)
2 teaspoons sea salt
1 teaspoon ground turmeric
1 teaspoon chilli powder *or* paprika
100 ml/3½ fl oz water
3 tablespoons caster sugar

Fried green tomatoes

1 Slice tomatoes lengthwise into eighths. **2** Heat oil in a large frying pan and add onion and GREEN MASALA PASTE. Cook gently for a few minutes. **3** Add tomato and stir to coat thoroughly with spice paste. Cook over moderate heat for 5 minutes until tomato begins to soften, tossing pan occasionally to prevent sticking. **4** Add salt, turmeric and chilli and toss to combine. Add water and sugar and cook for a further 10 minutes or until water has evaporated. **5** Taste and, if necessary, adjust seasoning. Serve warm.

Serves 4

200 g/6½ oz thick plain yoghurt
1 teaspoon ground turmeric
2 teaspoons coriander seeds, roasted and ground
4 teaspoons GREEN MASALA PASTE (page 142)
1 tablespoon shredded mint leaves
2 tablespoons chickpea flour/besan
4 chicken thighs, cut in half at the joint
2 tablespoons ghee
2 medium-size brown onions, finely sliced
3 teaspoons fish sauce
2 tablespoons flaked almonds, lightly toasted
extra shredded mint leaves

Mint and yoghurt chicken

1 In a bowl, mix yoghurt with turmeric, ground coriander, GREEN MASALA PASTE, mint and flour. Add chicken and marinate, covered, at room temperature for 1 hour. **2** In a wide-based pan, melt ghee and fry onion over moderate heat for about 5 minutes, or until it begins to colour. **3** Remove chicken from marinade and fry in pan with onion until chicken begins to colour. Add marinade, reduce heat to low and cook for about 25 minutes, or until chicken is tender. **4** Add fish sauce and cook for another 5 minutes. Taste and, if necessary, adjust seasoning. When chicken is cooked, transfer to a serving plate and sprinkle with almonds and extra mint.

Serves 4

Coriander Peanut Pesto

This is an Asian version of the more familiar Italian basil pesto, fired up with a touch of chilli and some aromatic herbs. Its flavour is redolent of the Orient, with a fresh, heady zing on the palate. Spoon it over hot noodles or pasta, serve it as a condiment with won tons or dumplings or stir it into soups. Like its Italian cousin, this pesto has maximum flavour impact when fresh, so it is best made when there is an abundance of fresh herbs available. Be sure that the peanuts you use are as fresh as possible – taste them in their raw state to double-check – because rancid nuts are not pleasant on the palate. Do not substitute Italian basil pesto in the following recipes; they are specifically designed to partner coriander peanut pesto.

Coriander peanut pesto

200 ml/6½ fl oz peanut oil
40 g/1¼ oz raw peanuts, blanched
2 green birds-eye chillies, finely chopped
1 tablespoon finely chopped ginger
8 cloves garlic, finely chopped
2 firmly packed cups Thai/holy basil leaves
½ firmly packed cup Vietnamese mint/laksa leaves
2 firmly packed cups coriander/cilantro/
   Chinese parsley leaves
1 teaspoon shaved palm sugar/jaggery
2 teaspoons fish sauce
20 ml/¾ fl oz strained lime juice

1 Heat oil in a frying pan and fry peanuts over moderate heat until golden. Strain peanuts, reserving oil, and allow to cool. **2** Blend cooled peanuts in a food processor with chilli, ginger and garlic. Add herbs and half the reserved oil, and blend to a smooth paste. **3** Blend in palm sugar, fish sauce and lime juice and process until herbs are finely chopped. **4** With motor running, gradually pour in enough of the remaining oil to make a smooth paste. Spoon into a sterilised jar, cover with a film of oil and seal. Keeps, refrigerated, for up to 2 weeks, but is best used soon after it is made.

Makes about 400 ml/13 fl oz

1 × 200 g/6½ oz eggplant/aubergine
1 red capsicum/bell pepper
1 yellow capsicum/bell pepper
2 small (pencil) leeks, trimmed
2 small zucchini/courgettes, sliced lengthwise
2 small waxy potatoes, peeled and sliced
1 large red/Spanish onion, sliced into thick rings
8 asparagus spears, trimmed and peeled
olive oil
4 teaspoons sea salt
2 teaspoons freshly ground black pepper
4 teaspoons coriander seeds, roasted and ground
½ cup coriander/cilantro/Chinese parsley leaves
4 tablespoons CORIANDER PEANUT PESTO (page 154)

Grilled vegetables with coriander

1 Cut eggplant lengthwise into 1 cm/½ in slices. Lightly salt and set aside on a tray for 30 minutes. **2** Roast capsicums over direct flame to blacken skins. Peel, discard seeds and slice flesh into thick strips. **3** Heat a cast-iron grill pan or barbecue. Brush each piece of vegetable with olive oil. Lay vegetables on a large tray and sprinkle generously with salt, pepper and ground coriander. **4** Grill vegetables, turning them halfway through cooking time, for 10–15 minutes or until softened and cooked. **5** Pile grilled vegetables onto a large, warm plate and sprinkle with coriander leaves. Pass CORIANDER PEANUT PESTO as a condiment for dipping.

Serves 4

200 g/6½ oz fresh Chinese egg noodles *or*
  spaghettini pasta
olive oil
24 large Pacific oysters, unshucked
50 g/1½ oz tatsoi leaves/*or* small leaves Chinese white
  cabbage/bok choy
2 teaspoons pickled ginger, finely sliced
½ cup coriander/cilantro/Chinese parsley leaves
4 green onions/scallions, cut into 1 cm/½ in lengths
1 large green chilli, finely sliced
100 g/3½ oz snow pea sprouts
4 teaspoons CORIANDER PEANUT PESTO (page 154)
Oyster dressing
100 ml/3½ fl oz Fish Stock (page 201)
20 ml/¾ fl oz Tamarind Liquid (page 200)
40 ml/1¼ fl oz reserved oyster juices, strained
1 teaspoon fish sauce
1 teaspoon light soy sauce
2 teaspoons mirin
2 teaspoons strained lime juice

Pacific oysters stir-fried with coriander noodles

1 Blanch noodles briefly in boiling water, then drain and dress with a little olive oil to prevent sticking. **2** Shuck oysters and reserve juices for dressing. Discard shells. **3** To make oyster dressing, mix all ingredients in a bowl. Taste for balance between acid and salt and adjust if necessary. Set aside. **4** Divide all ingredients into 4 portions. For each serve, put a portion of noodles, tatsoi leaves and dressing into a bowl and remaining ingredients into another bowl – you should have 2 bowls for each person (8 in total). Each portion must be cooked separately to ensure perfect cooking. **5** Stand wok (or woks, if you have more than one) over high heat and tip in first portion of noodles, dressing and tatsoi. Toss until warmed through, being careful that noodles don't stick. Add second bowl of ingredients, stirring with tongs to combine quickly, and toss over heat until warmed through, about 1 minute. Pile onto a plate and serve immediately. **6** Repeat process until all portions are cooked. The number of repeats depends on the number of woks you have. Even if you have only one, the cooking is so quick that the cooked portions can wait without loss of heat or quality while the remaining portions are cooked.

Serves 4

Spiced coconut broth with shellfish and coriander

2 blue swimmer crabs, cleaned and split in half
4 large green king prawns/shrimp, shelled and deveined
12 black mussels, steamed open
2 × 200 g/6½ oz marron tails, split in half
8 fresh sea scallops
8 Chinese white cabbage/bok choy hearts, blanched
½ cup coriander/cilantro/Chinese parsley leaves
1 teaspoon finely sliced rounds of red birds-eye chilli
2 kaffir lime leaves, shredded
4 teaspoons CORIANDER PEANUT PESTO (page 154)
4 teaspoons Fried Shallot Slices (page 201)

Spiced coconut broth
800 ml/26 fl oz coconut milk
1 tablespoon finely chopped fresh galangal
2 teaspoons finely chopped ginger
3 red birds-eye chillies, finely chopped
2 coriander/cilantro/Chinese parsley roots, finely chopped
4 red shallots, sliced lengthwise
4 kaffir lime leaves, shredded
2 stalks lemongrass, finely chopped
rind/zest of 1 kaffir lime
400 ml/12½ fl oz Prawn/Shrimp Stock (page 202)
50 ml/1½ fl oz fish sauce
40 ml/1¼ fl oz strained lime juice

1 To make spiced coconut broth, bring coconut milk to the boil in a saucepan, uncovered, and boil for a few minutes. Add aromatics and simmer for a few minutes. Add stock and fish sauce and simmer on low heat for 15 minutes. Pass broth through a fine mesh sieve and add lime juice. Taste and, if necessary, adjust seasoning. **2** Butterfly prawns open by cutting down their backs and flattening them. Remove mussels from shells and discard shells. **3** Reheat broth in a wide-based pan and when it starts to boil, add crab. Reduce heat to very low and simmer for 3 minutes. Add prawns and marron tails and cook, stirring occasionally, for 3 minutes. Add scallops and mussels and cook for 2 minutes. Remove shellfish from pan with a slotted spoon and place on a warm plate. **4** Add blanched Chinese white cabbage hearts to broth and reheat for 1 minute to warm through. **5** Spoon 2 Chinese white cabbage hearts into centre of 4 serving bowls and divide shellfish between bowls. **6** Stir coriander, chilli and lime leaves into broth and ladle over shellfish. **7** Add a teaspoon of CORIANDER PEANUT PESTO to each serve and, using a chopstick, swirl into broth. Sprinkle with fried shallot slices and serve.

Serves 4

Note: Fish Stock (page 201) can be used instead of Prawn/Shrimp Stock.

vegetable oil, for deep-frying
8 small fish fillets
8 snow peas, trimmed
4 round slices eggplant/aubergine
½ green capsicum/bell pepper, cut into quarters
8 asparagus tips
1 cup Tempura Batter (page 201)
16 teaspoons CORIANDER PEANUT PESTO (page 154)
80 ml/2½ fl oz extra-virgin olive oil

Fish and vegetable tempura with coriander peanut pesto

1 Heat vegetable oil in a deep-fryer or large pot to 180°C/350°F. **2** Dip fish pieces and vegetables in tempura batter and fry quickly, in small batches, in hot oil for 2–3 minutes or until crispy. Remove with a slotted spoon and set aside to drain on paper towel. Repeat until all fish and vegetables have been cooked. **3** Mix CORIANDER PEANUT PESTO with olive oil and place in dipping bowls. Arrange fish and vegetables on plates and serve immediately.

Serves 4

Roasted chicken and coriander fennel salad

2 teaspoons finely chopped coriander/cilantro/
  Chinese parsley roots
2 teaspoons finely chopped garlic
80 ml/2½ fl oz olive oil
1 teaspoon freshly ground black pepper
1 teaspoon sea salt
1 teaspoon fish sauce
8 green onions/scallions, finely sliced
1 × 2 kg/4½ lb chicken
2 fennel bulbs, finely shaved
½ cup coriander/cilantro/Chinese parsley leaves
200 g/6½ oz snow pea sprouts
4 teaspoons CORIANDER PEANUT PESTO (page 154)

1 Preheat oven to hot (220°C/450°F). Mix coriander root with garlic, oil, pepper, sea salt, fish sauce and half the green onion. Push some of this paste between skin and meat of chicken and rub the remainder into cavity and over all surfaces. **2** Truss chicken and place in an oiled roasting tray. Roast for 1 hour, or until chicken is golden and juices run clear when thigh is pierced with a skewer. Remove chicken from tray and set aside in a warm place. **3** Add remaining green onion, fennel, coriander leaves, snow pea sprouts and CORIANDER PEANUT PESTO to the juices in the tray. Toss to combine until leaves have wilted. **4** Place warm salad on plates. Carve chicken and add to the salad. Serve immediately.

Serves 4

Chicken and coriander broth

1.2 litres/38 fl oz White Chicken Stock (page 202)
2 chicken breasts
80 ml/2½ fl oz light soy sauce
½ teaspoon sea salt
½ teaspoon freshly ground white pepper
4 eggs, lightly beaten
200 g/6½ oz bean sprouts
1 tablespoon finely sliced ginger
1 cup watercress leaves
½ cup coriander/cilantro/Chinese parsley leaves
16 teaspoons CORIANDER PEANUT PESTO (page 154)

1 Bring stock to boiling point in a saucepan. Add chicken, cover with a lid and turn off heat. Leave chicken in hot stock for 20 minutes, then remove and shred meat. **2** Return stock to the boil and flavour with soy sauce, salt and pepper. **3** Stir egg into boiling stock, swirling with a chopstick to form threads. Remove saucepan from heat. **4** Put shredded chicken, bean sprouts, ginger, watercress and coriander leaves into bowls and ladle broth over. Swirl 4 teaspoons CORIANDER PEANUT PESTO into each bowl and serve.
Serves 4

Note: To make this soup heartier, add cooked noodles of your choice – somen, thin egg noodles, rice noodles or angel hair pasta.

20 ml/¾ fl oz peanut oil

2 cloves garlic, minced

1 large red Chinese *or* Dutch chilli, finely sliced

400 ml/12½ fl oz Fish Stock (page 201) *or* water

½ cup Chinese Shaoxing rice wine

40 ml/1¼ fl oz fish sauce

2 kg/4½ lb clams, scrubbed and soaked in cold water
  (see Note)

4 teaspoons CORIANDER PEANUT PESTO (page 154)

1 cup coriander/cilantro/Chinese parsley leaves

1 cup snow pea sprouts, trimmed

3 green onions/scallions, finely sliced

100 g/3½ oz somen noodles, cooked and drained

1 teaspoon chilli oil

Clams tossed with coriander pesto and chilli oil

1 Heat peanut oil in a large, heavy-based pot over medium heat. Fry garlic and chilli for a few seconds until fragrant. Add stock, rice wine and fish sauce. Cover and bring to the boil. Add clams, cover and bring back to the boil. **2** Reduce heat to a simmer and cook for 5–6 minutes or until clams open. Taste and, if necessary, adjust seasoning. Remove from heat and stir in CORIANDER PEANUT PESTO, coriander leaves, snow pea sprouts and green onion. **3** Divide noodles equally between 4 serving bowls and drizzle with a little chilli oil. Ladle clams and their broth over noodles and serve immediately.

Serves 4

Note: Mussels can be substituted for the clams. They need to be washed and de-bearded before cooking.

Massaman Curry Paste

Massaman curry paste is specific to central and southern Thailand and translates as 'Muslim curry'. It is named after the Malay traders who influenced the foods of the region over the past century. In their turn, they were directly influenced by migrating Indians, so the food has a mixed ancestry. Curries made with this paste are complex, rich and spicy and the inclusion of the Indian spices cardamom and cinnamon provides a wonderful depth of flavour. The paste is usually cooked into coconut cream with thinner coconut milk added at a later stage, along with roasted peanuts. For best results, use with chicken and beef or other rich, red meats. The paste also makes a good base for a spicy, stock-based sauce or a stir-fry, and can transform a marinade.

Massaman curry paste

4 teaspoons cumin seeds
8 teaspoons coriander seeds
seeds from 5 green cardamom pods
6 cloves
2 sticks cinnamon
8 dried birds-eye chillies
2 teaspoons Thai shrimp paste/kapi
6 red birds-eye chillies, chopped
20 cloves garlic, chopped
2 small brown onions, chopped
4 teaspoons fresh green peppercorns
5 coriander/cilantro/Chinese parsley roots, chopped
50 ml/1½ fl oz vegetable oil
rind/zest of 2 kaffir limes, finely chopped
2 stalks lemongrass, chopped
75 g/2½ oz palm sugar/jaggery, shaved
80 ml/2½ fl oz fish sauce
60 ml/2 fl oz Tamarind Liquid (page 200)

1 Dry-roast cumin, coriander and cardamom seeds with cloves, cinnamon sticks and dried chillies over gentle heat until fragrant. Cool, then grind to a fine powder. **2** Dry-roast shrimp paste over gentle heat until fragrant. **3** Blend fresh chilli, garlic, onion, peppercorns, coriander root and vegetable oil to a fine paste in a food processor. Cook paste over gentle heat in a frying pan until slightly coloured and softened. **4** Return hot paste to food processor and blend with lime rind, lemongrass and dry-roasted shrimp paste. **5** Mix paste, ground spices and remaining ingredients thoroughly. Spoon into a sterilised jar, cover with a film of oil and seal when cool. Keeps, refrigerated, for 2 weeks.

Makes about 250 ml/8 fl oz

200 ml/6½ fl oz coconut cream

1 tablespoon shaved palm sugar/jaggery

20 ml/¾ fl oz fish sauce

2 teaspoons MASSAMAN CURRY PASTE (page 166)

2 teaspoons SAMBAL BAJAK (page 42)

2 teaspoons strained lime juice

24 fresh sea scallops, cleaned

1 large red Chinese *or* Dutch chilli, seeded and
   finely sliced

¼ cup freshly shaved *or* grated coconut

2 green onions/scallions, sliced

4 kaffir lime leaves, shredded

4 tablespoons shredded segments of pomelo *or*
   ruby grapefruit

1 small cucumber, seeded and finely sliced

2 tablespoons coriander/cilantro/Chinese parsley leaves

2 tablespoons shredded Thai/holy basil leaves

¼ cup watercress leaves

2 tablespoons Fried Shallot Slices (page 201)

Coconut chilli scallops with pomelo salad

1 Bring coconut cream, palm sugar and fish sauce to the boil in a saucepan, uncovered, then reduce to a simmer and stir in MASSAMAN CURRY PASTE, SAMBAL BAJAK and lime juice. Cook for 5 minutes. Taste and, if necessary, adjust seasoning. **2** Reduce heat to very low and poach scallops in coconut sauce for 2–3 minutes. Remove scallops from sauce and remove sauce from heat. **3** Mix all remaining ingredients, except fried shallot slices, in a bowl. Add scallops and coconut sauce and toss to combine. **4** Pile warm scallop salad onto serving plates, positioning scallops on top. Sprinkle with fried shallots and serve immediately.

Serves 4

2 × 1 kg/2 lb live rock lobsters (see Note)

8 teaspoons MASSAMAN CURRY PASTE (page 166)

1 teaspoon CHILLI JAM (page 6)

200 ml/6½ fl oz coconut milk

50 ml/1½ fl oz tomato purée

30 ml/1 fl oz fish sauce

8 fresh banana leaves

¼ cup Fried Shallot Slices (page 201)

2 large red Chinese *or* Dutch chillies, split lengthwise,
seeded and deep-fried

Spicy masala lobster

1 Stun lobsters in freezer for 30 minutes, then plunge briefly into a stockpot of rapidly boiling water (this is to kill rather than cook them). **2** Remove lobster tail meat and discard heads, shells and claws (use them to make stock for another recipe). Cut each lobster tail in half lengthwise. **3** Preheat oven to moderately hot (200°C/400°F). **4** Bring MASSAMAN CURRY PASTE, CHILLI JAM, coconut milk, tomato purée and fish sauce to a simmer in a saucepan, stirring to combine. Allow to cool. **5** Coat lobster liberally with cooled sauce and pile into tail halves. Wrap each piece of tail in a banana leaf, folding over to secure. **6** Bake the 4 parcels seam-side down for 8–10 minutes, or until meat is just cooked. Unwrap and spoon a little sauce over lobster to moisten it. **7** Spread remaining banana leaves on 4 plates, add a masala lobster tail and its sauce to each plate and garnish with fried shallots and deep-fried chilli. Serve immediately.

Serves 4

Note: This recipe also works with bug tail meat (slipper lobster), Australian marron tails, crayfish and langoustines.

300 ml/10 fl oz coconut milk
150 ml/5 fl oz Fish Stock (page 201)
20 ml/¾ fl oz fish sauce
8 teaspoons MASSAMAN CURRY PASTE (page 166)
2 teaspoons CHILLI JAM (page 6)
2 teaspoons strained lime juice
4 × 150 g/5 oz white fish fillets
½ cup coriander/cilantro/Chinese parsley leaves
steamed rice *or* stir-fried green vegetables, to serve

Steamed fish with red chilli paste

1 In a saucepan, heat coconut milk, stock, fish sauce, MASSAMAN CURRY PASTE and CHILLI JAM together to boiling point, uncovered. Simmer for 5 minutes. Remove from heat and stir in lime juice. Taste and, if necessary, adjust seasoning. Allow to cool completely. **2** Place fish fillets in a large, shallow bowl in a single layer and pour over half the cooled sauce. Place bowl in a large steamer tray, cover with a lid and steam over boiling water for 8–12 minutes, depending on the size and type of fish used. Test fish with a skewer or knife to check that it is cooked. The flesh should be white and firm without being dry or breaking open. **3** Boil remaining sauce in a saucepan, uncovered, for 5 minutes. **4** Carefully slide fish fillets onto plates, spoon sauce over and top with coriander leaves. Serve with steamed rice or stir-fried green vegetables. A spicy rice pilaf or wilted spinach are also good accompaniments.

Serves 4

4 chicken thighs, cut in half at the joint
2 teaspoons Chinese Five-spice Powder (page 200)
1 teaspoon sea salt
40 ml/1¼ fl oz vegetable oil
8 red *or* golden shallots, peeled
300 ml/10 fl oz coconut cream
8 teaspoons MASSAMAN CURRY PASTE (page 166)
300 ml/10 fl oz Brown Chicken Stock (page 202)
20 ml/¾ fl oz fish sauce
40 ml/1¼ fl oz Tamarind Liquid (page 200)
1 tablespoon shaved palm sugar/jaggery
8 small waxy potatoes, peeled and halved
2 tablespoons peanuts, blanched and roughly chopped
½ cup Thai/holy basil leaves
steamed rice and pickled vegetables, to serve

Chicken and potato curry

1 Season chicken with five-spice powder and salt. Heat oil in a large saucepan and fry chicken on both sides for about 6 minutes, or until browned. Set aside. **2** In the same pan, fry whole shallots until they begin to colour. Add coconut cream and bring to the boil. Simmer for a few minutes until coconut cream appears oily, then stir in MASSAMAN CURRY PASTE and simmer gently for a further 5 minutes. **3** Add stock, fish sauce, tamarind liquid and palm sugar and bring to the boil. Add potato and simmer for 10 minutes. **4** Add browned chicken, cover and cook for another 40 minutes on low heat, or until chicken is tender and potato is soft. Stir occasionally to ensure meat is kept coated with sauce. **5** Stir in peanuts and basil and serve with steamed rice and pickled vegetables.

Serves 4

4 large quails
8 teaspoons MASSAMAN CURRY PASTE (page 166)
vegetable oil, for deep-frying
200 g/6½ oz small spinach leaves
2 cloves garlic, finely chopped
2 teaspoons fish sauce
½ teaspoon freshly ground black pepper
2 tablespoons Fried Shallot Slices (page 201)

Deep-fried spiced quails

1 Preheat oven to hot (220°C/450°F). Wash quails and pat dry with paper towel. Rub MASSAMAN CURRY PASTE into cavity of each bird and onto outer surfaces, covering generously. **2** Heat oil in a deep-fryer or large pot to 180°C/350°F. Deep-fry quails for 4 minutes. Transfer to a baking tray and bake for a further 3 minutes. Remove quails from oven and rest for 2 minutes before serving. **3** Stir-fry spinach in a little oil with garlic, fish sauce and pepper for about 1 minute, or until wilted. **4** Place some spinach in the centre of each serving plate, sit a quail on top and sprinkle with fried shallot slices to serve.

Serves 4

Rich beef curry

20 ml/¾ fl oz vegetable oil
2 medium-size brown onions, finely sliced lengthwise
4 cloves garlic, sliced
2 small red birds-eye *or* serrano chillies, sliced
800 ml/26 fl oz coconut milk
12 teaspoons MASSAMAN CURRY PASTE (page 166)
1 stalk lemongrass, cut into 5 cm/2 in lengths
2 kaffir lime leaves
2 teaspoons ground turmeric
80 ml/2½ fl oz Tamarind Liquid (page 200)
40 ml/1¼ fl oz light soy sauce
1 kg/2 lb chuck *or* blade steak, cut in 5 cm/2 in cubes
200 g/6½ oz pumpkin, cut into 2.5 cm/1 in cubes
20 ml/¾ fl oz fish sauce
½ cup coriander/cilantro/Chinese parsley leaves
steamed rice, to serve

1 Heat oil in a large pot and fry onion, garlic and chilli until beginning to colour. **2** Add coconut milk, MASSAMAN CURRY PASTE, lemongrass, lime leaves, turmeric, tamarind liquid and soy sauce. Bring to the boil and simmer, uncovered, for 5 minutes. **3** Add meat and cook, stirring regularly, on very gentle heat for 1 hour. **4** Add pumpkin and, if too much of the sauce has been absorbed, a little water. Cook for another hour or until pumpkin is soft and the curry is quite dry in appearance, with most of the liquid having been absorbed by the meat. **5** Season with fish sauce. Taste and, if necessary, adjust seasoning. **6** Sprinkle with coriander leaves and serve with steamed rice.

Serves 4

Note: The longer and slower you cook this curry, the better its flavour and texture. And, like most curries, it is even better made a day or two in advance and reheated gently to serve.

1 small brown onion, finely chopped

2 cloves garlic, finely chopped

1 teaspoon finely chopped fresh galangal

1 teaspoon chilli powder *or* paprika

2 teaspoons Garam Masala (page 200)

2 teaspoons sea salt

1 teaspoon freshly ground black pepper

600 g/1 lb 3 oz lean minced beef *or* lamb

2 tablespoons finely chopped flat-leaf parsley

1 tablespoon coriander/cilantro/Chinese parsley
   leaves, chopped

1 egg

2 tablespoons breadcrumbs

plain/all-purpose flour, for dusting

Curry sauce

100 ml/3½ fl oz coconut cream

100 ml/3½ fl oz tomato purée

8 teaspoons MASSAMAN CURRY PASTE (page 166)

2 teaspoons CHILLI JAM (page 6)

300 ml/10 fl oz Beef/Veal Stock (page 203)

2 teaspoons light soy sauce

2 teaspoons fish sauce

2 teaspoons strained lime juice

Spiced meatballs with curry sauce

1 To make meatballs, blend onion, garlic, galangal, dry spices, salt, pepper, meat, herbs, egg and breadcrumbs in a food processor until smooth and combined. Roll into small balls and then roll each ball in a little flour to prevent sticking. **2** To make sauce, heat coconut cream with tomato purée, MASSAMAN CURRY PASTE and CHILLI JAM and bring to the boil. Cook for 10 minutes, uncovered, on moderate heat. Add stock, soy sauce and fish sauce and simmer for 20 minutes. Add lime juice. Taste and, if necessary, adjust seasoning. Strain sauce through muslin or a fine mesh sieve and discard solids. Pour into a clean pot. **3** Heat a little oil in a large frying pan and fry meatballs in batches for about 10 minutes, or until well browned on all sides. Add meatballs to curry sauce and cook, stirring occasionally, over low heat for 15 minutes. Serve with a rice pilaf or steamed rice.

Serves 4

Green Curry Paste

Each curry paste will vary according to its specific ingredients and the way it is put together. The green curry paste made under my label is quite mild and easy on the palate, and fragrant because of the aromatic green herbs used in its preparation. It can be used in a multitude of ways, as these recipes will demonstrate, and, of course, you can also use it with your own personal favourite dishes. You can control the heat by varying the type and size of chillies you use. If you want to reduce the heat even further, discard the chilli seeds when making the paste.

Green curry paste

1 teaspoon Thai shrimp paste/kapi
1 teaspoon coriander seeds
½ teaspoon cumin seeds
20 green birds-eye chillies, roughly chopped
5 golden shallots, chopped
6 cloves garlic, chopped
2 stalks lemongrass, chopped
4 teaspoons chopped fresh galangal
8 teaspoons chopped fresh coriander/cilantro/
  Chinese parsley root
½ cup coriander/cilantro/Chinese parsley leaves
¼ cup Thai/holy basil leaves
1 teaspoon chopped kaffir lime rind/zest
3 teaspoons fresh green peppercorns
¼ teaspoon freshly grated nutmeg
2 teaspoons fish sauce
4 teaspoons water

1 Dry-roast shrimp paste, coriander seeds and cumin seeds separately over gentle heat until fragrant. Cool, then combine and grind to a fine powder. **2** Blend all ingredients to a fine paste in a food processor. Spoon into a sterilised jar, cover with a film of oil and seal when cool. Keeps, refrigerated, for up to 2 weeks. *Makes 200 ml/6½ fl oz*

500 g/1 lb mixed green vegetables (asparagus, beans, snow peas, broccoli, zucchini/courgettes – whatever is in season)
1 bunch spinach
8 fresh beancurd/tofu squares
300 ml/10 fl oz coconut milk
8 teaspoons GREEN CURRY PASTE (page 178)
8 kaffir lime leaves
300 ml/10 fl oz Spiced Vegetable Stock (page 204)
20 ml/¾ fl oz fish sauce
2 teaspoons strained lime juice
½ cup Thai/holy basil leaves
½ cup coriander/cilantro/Chinese parsley leaves
boiled *or* steamed rice, to serve

Green vegetable curry with beancurd

1 Prepare green vegetables by slicing or cutting into uniform thickness to ensure even cooking. Wash spinach in cold water and remove and discard stalks. Cut each beancurd square into quarters. **2** Heat coconut milk to boiling point in a saucepan and stir in GREEN CURRY PASTE and lime leaves. Simmer gently, uncovered, for 5 minutes. Add stock, fish sauce and lime juice and simmer for a further 10 minutes. Taste and, if necessary, adjust seasoning. **3** Add prepared vegetables and cook for 6–10 minutes, or until vegetables are soft but not mushy. Add spinach leaves and allow to wilt in the sauce. **4** Carefully stir in beancurd pieces with basil and coriander leaves. Heat through for 2 minutes, then serve with boiled or steamed rice.

Serves 4

Turmeric lemongrass broth with noodles and vegetables

200 g/6½ oz fresh Egg Noodles (page 204) *or* ramen noodles *or* purchased egg noodles

2 large red Chinese *or* Dutch chillies, seeded and finely sliced

1 zucchini/courgette, cut into julienne

6 green onions/scallions, finely sliced

100 g/3½ oz bean sprouts

1 small carrot, peeled and cut into julienne

4 shiitake mushrooms, finely sliced

4 teaspoons finely shredded mint leaves

Turmeric lemongrass broth

8 teaspoons GREEN CURRY PASTE (page 178)

2 teaspoons finely chopped ginger

1 stalk lemongrass, chopped

2 teaspoons ground turmeric

2 teaspoons vegetable oil

1 litre/32 fl oz Spiced Vegetable Stock (page 204)

200 ml/6½ fl oz Tamarind Liquid (page 200)

80 ml/2½ fl oz light soy sauce

2 teaspoons lemon juice, strained

60 ml/2 fl oz Sugar Syrup (page 201) *or* 2 tablespoons caster sugar

1 teaspoon freshly ground white pepper

1 To make broth, fry GREEN CURRY PASTE, ginger, lemongrass and turmeric in vegetable oil for 5 minutes, or until fragrant. Add remaining broth ingredients, except pepper, and bring to the boil. Reduce heat and simmer for 10 minutes. Strain through a fine mesh sieve and discard solids. Reheat broth in a clean pot and stir in pepper. **2** Cook noodles in boiling water, then drain and divide between 4 bowls. Combine chilli and vegetables and add to noodles. Ladle hot broth into bowls to cover noodles and vegetables. Stir with a chopstick. **3** Sprinkle mint on top and serve immediately.

Serves 4

Green curry fish soup

500 ml/16 fl oz coconut milk

8 teaspoons GREEN CURRY PASTE (page 178)

750 ml/24 fl oz Fish Stock (page 201) *or* water

40 ml/1¼ fl oz fish sauce

4 white fish fillets, cut into thick strips

20 small prawns/shrimp, shelled and deveined

12 fish balls (available from Asian food stores)

2 tablespoons coriander/cilantro/Chinese parsley leaves

4 kaffir lime leaves, finely shredded

1 tablespoon shredded mint leaves

8 Whole Roasted Shallots (red) (page 201)

250 g/8 oz bean sprouts

1 Heat coconut milk to boiling point. Stir in GREEN CURRY PASTE and cook for 5 minutes on moderate heat, uncovered. Add stock and fish sauce. Bring to the boil, reduce heat and simmer for 15 minutes. Taste and, if necessary, adjust seasoning. **2** Add fish pieces, prawns and fish balls and simmer on very low heat for 3–4 minutes, just enough to cook the fish. **3** Remove fish, prawns and fish balls from pot with a slotted spoon and divide between 4 bowls. Distribute remaining ingredients between bowls, pour hot soup over and serve.

Serves 4

sea salt

500 g/1 lb belly pork *or* spareribs, cut into 5 cm/2 in strips

20 ml/¾ fl oz vegetable oil

8 teaspoons GREEN CURRY PASTE (page 178)

4 kaffir lime leaves

2 stalks lemongrass, cut into 5 cm/2 in lengths

4 slices fresh galangal

1 teaspoon minced ginger

625 ml/20 fl oz coconut milk

100 ml/3 fl oz Tamarind Liquid (page 200)

2 teaspoons shaved palm sugar/jaggery

20 ml/¾ fl oz fish sauce

2 small green jalapeño chillies, seeded and sliced

½ cup coriander/cilantro/Chinese parsley leaves

8 Whole Roasted Shallots (page 201)

steamed rice, to serve

Green curry of pork

1 Rub salt lightly into pork and refrigerate on a covered tray for 1 hour. **2** Blanch pork in boiling water for 2 minutes, then remove from pot with a slotted spoon and set aside. **3** Heat oil in a wok over high heat and fry GREEN CURRY PASTE, lime leaves, lemongrass, galangal and ginger, stirring constantly, for 2 minutes or until mixture begins to colour. Add pork and coat thoroughly with paste. **4** Stir in coconut milk, tamarind liquid, palm sugar and fish sauce. Reduce heat to low and simmer, uncovered and stirring occasionally, for 25–30 minutes or until pork is tender and liquid has evaporated slightly. **5** Add chilli, coriander leaves and roasted shallots. Taste and, if necessary, adjust seasoning. Serve with steamed rice.

Serves 4

Note: Belly pork (as opposed to a leaner cut like shoulder or neck) is necessary for this dish as a fair degree of fat is needed to give a tender final result.

250 ml/8 fl oz coconut cream
4 teaspoons GREEN CURRY PASTE (page 178)
2 teaspoons fish sauce
200 ml/6½ fl oz Prawn/Shrimp Stock (page 202)
16 green tiger prawns/large shrimp, shelled
1 cup Thai basil leaves, shredded
150 g/5 oz small spinach leaves, washed
2 teaspoons olive oil

Tiger prawns with green coconut curry

1 Heat coconut cream to simmering point, stir in GREEN CURRY PASTE and fish sauce and cook over moderate heat for 10 minutes. **2** Add stock and bring to the boil. Simmer for 10 minutes. Taste and, if necessary, adjust seasoning. **3** Add prawns to sauce and simmer on low heat for 3–4 minutes, just long enough so the prawns change colour without overcooking and toughening. **4** Add basil leaves. **5** Wilt spinach in a pan with oil and place on centre of plates. Sit prawns on top and spoon sauce over.

Serves 4

3 litres/96 fl oz White Chicken Stock (page 202)
1 teaspoon sea salt
1 teaspoon freshly ground white pepper
1 × 1.8 kg/4 lb free-range chicken
2 green onions/scallions
3 slices ginger
250 ml/8 fl oz coconut milk
8 teaspoons GREEN CURRY PASTE (page 178)
2 teaspoons fish sauce
200 g/6½ oz small spinach leaves, washed
1 bunch Chinese celery/kun choy *or* plain celery
½ cup coriander/cilantro/Chinese parsley leaves

White-cooked chicken with green curry sauce

1 Heat stock to boiling point in a large pot. Rub salt and pepper into skin and cavity of chicken and stuff green onions and ginger into cavity. Tie legs together with string. **2** Place trussed chicken into hot stock, turn off heat and leave to cook slowly in the stock for 1 hour. Check thigh joint with a skewer – if juices run pale pink, the chicken is ready. If not quite ready, leave in the stock a little longer. Remove chicken from pot and set aside in a warm place. Strain stock through a fine mesh sieve or muslin and set aside. **3** Heat coconut milk to boiling point, stir in GREEN CURRY PASTE and fish sauce and cook for 5 minutes, uncovered. Add 200 ml/6½ fl oz of reserved stock and cook for a further 10 minutes. (Keep remaining stock for another use.) Taste and, if necessary, adjust seasoning. **4** Joint chicken, then cut meat from the bones into thick slices. **5** Bring a saucepan of water to the boil and blanch spinach leaves and celery until wilted, about 30 seconds. Squeeze dry, then divide between 4 plates. Spoon over the green curry sauce. Sit a few slices of chicken on top of spinach, sprinkle with coriander leaves and serve immediately.

Serves 4

Red Curry Paste

Like the green and Massaman curry pastes, this fragrant, sweet and spicy curry paste draws its inspiration and unique flavour combination from Thailand. The flavours have become so familiar in Australia that they are now considered by most people to be a staple in the pantry. For the intriguing depth of flavour of this paste, it is essential that you include Thai shrimp paste/kapi. This single ingredient gives the paste its unique and mysterious pungency. Apart from its obvious uses, try using red curry paste for grilling, or spiking the flavour of meatballs or a baked meatloaf, or as a marinade or to add flavour to a soup. Like its green counterpart, its heat intensity varies according to the number and size of chillies used, so the outcome can be controlled by the maker. Add a few extra chillies if you prefer your paste fiery-hot.

Red curry paste

6 large dried Chinese *or* cayenne chillies, chopped
50 ml/1½ fl oz warm water
2 teaspoons Thai shrimp paste/kapi
1 teaspoon coriander seeds
½ teaspoon white peppercorns, ground
6 red shallots, chopped
6 red birds-eye chillies, finely chopped
6 cloves garlic, chopped
2 teaspoons finely chopped ginger
1 tablespoon finely chopped fresh galangal
1 stalk lemongrass, chopped
1 teaspoon finely chopped kaffir lime rind/zest
1 tablespoon chopped coriander/cilantro/
   Chinese parsley root
4 teaspoons CHILLI JAM (page 6)
30 ml/1 fl oz fish sauce

1 Soak dried chilli in warm water for 15 minutes. **2** Meanwhile, dry-roast shrimp paste and coriander seeds separately over gentle heat until fragrant. Cool, then grind coriander seeds to a fine powder. **3** Process all ingredients to a smooth paste in an electric blender or food processor. **4** Spoon into a sterilised jar, cover with a film of oil and seal. Keeps, refrigerated, for 2 months.

Makes about 200 ml/6½ fl oz

1 cup chopped pineapple
1 teaspoon freshly ground black pepper
vegetable oil
8 teaspoons RED CURRY PASTE (page 188)
1 tablespoon shaved palm sugar/jaggery
400 ml/12½ fl oz coconut milk
100 ml/3½ fl oz Fish Stock (page 201) *or* water
24 large green tiger prawns/shrimp, shelled and deveined
20 ml/¾ fl oz fish sauce
½ cup shredded mint leaves
4 kaffir lime leaves, finely shredded
4 green onions/scallions, finely sliced
sticky white rice, to serve

Sweet prawn curry

1 Purée half the chopped pineapple and add pepper. Heat a little oil in a saucepan and fry RED CURRY PASTE, palm sugar and peppered pineapple for a few minutes, or until fragrant. **2** Add coconut milk and stock and bring to the boil. Simmer on low heat for 10 minutes, uncovered. **3** Add remaining chopped pineapple and simmer for 5 minutes. Add prawns and fish sauce and cook for 4–5 minutes, or until prawns are just cooked. Taste and, if necessary, adjust seasoning. **4** Stir in mint, lime leaves and green onion slices. Serve with sticky white rice.

Serves 4

Sautéd chilli prawns

20 ml/¾ fl oz vegetable oil
1 medium-size onion, sliced thickly lengthwise
1 teaspoon CHILLI JAM (page 6)
4 teaspoons RED CURRY PASTE (page 188)
20 cherry tomatoes
20 large green prawns/shrimp, shelled and deveined
20 ml/¾ fl oz strained lime juice
2 teaspoons fish sauce
2 tablespoons sugar
4 green onions/scallions, finely sliced
coconut rice/nasi lemak, to serve (see Note)

1 Heat oil in a large wok and fry onion until soft. Add CHILLI JAM and RED CURRY PASTE and cook for about 2 minutes. **2** Add tomatoes and prawns and toss over high heat until prawns begin to change colour. **3** Add lime juice, fish sauce and sugar and cook for another minute. Taste and, if necessary, adjust seasoning. Remove from heat and pile onto plates. **4** Sprinkle with green onion and serve with coconut rice.

Serves 4

Note: To make coconut rice, simply cook jasmine rice in the usual way but substitute coconut milk for water.

Fried Spanish mackerel with red curry sauce

250 ml/8 fl oz coconut cream

8 teaspoons RED CURRY PASTE (page 188)

2 teaspoons fish sauce

1 tablespoon dried shrimp, ground

1 teaspoon caster sugar

4 snake beans, cut into 2.5 cm/1 in lengths

2 red Chinese *or* Dutch chillies, finely sliced

vegetable oil, for deep-frying

600 g/1 lb 3 oz Spanish mackerel cutlets *or* fillets

2 tablespoons Thai/holy basil leaves

2 kaffir lime leaves, finely shredded

steamed rice, to serve

1 Heat coconut cream to simmering point in a saucepan. Add RED CURRY PASTE, fish sauce, dried shrimp and sugar. Stir. Cook for 10 minutes over moderate heat, uncovered. **2** Add beans and chilli and cook for another 3 minutes. Taste and, if necessary, adjust seasoning. **3** Heat oil to 180°C/350°F in a deep-fryer or large pot and fry fish pieces for 6–8 minutes, or until golden and crispy. Drain on paper towel. **4** To serve, place fish on 4 warmed plates and spoon sauce over. Scatter some basil leaves and lime leaves over top. Serve with steamed rice.

Serves 4

1 × 1.5 kg/3 lb whole fish, scaled and gutted
20 ml/¾ fl oz strained lime juice
½ teaspoon sea salt
½ teaspoon freshly ground black pepper
8 teaspoons RED CURRY PASTE (page 188)
4 teaspoons tomato purée
40 ml/1¼ fl oz vegetable oil
steamed *or* fried rice, to serve

Grilled spicy fish

1 With a sharp knife, cut a few diagonal slits about 2.5 cm/1 in deep into both sides of fish. (This ensures even cooking time and maximum penetration of spice paste during cooking.) Season inside cavity of fish with lime juice, salt and pepper. **2** Combine RED CURRY PASTE and tomato purée in a bowl. Fill inside cavity of fish with this and rub some over outer surfaces. Marinate for 2–3 hours. **3** Brush fish generously with oil to prevent sticking and place in a hinged wire fish griller (to keep fish together during cooking). Chargrill or barbecue over moderate heat for 12–14 minutes, turning fish after 8 minutes or so. Cooking time will depend on size and type of fish used. Check with a skewer at the thickest part of the flesh. It should be white and firm without being dry or breaking open. **4** Remove fish from heat, lift from the wire griller and transfer carefully to a serving plate (lined with a fresh banana leaf, if desired). Serve with steamed or fried rice.

Serves 4

Roasted duck and eggplant curry

200 ml/6½ fl oz coconut cream

8 teaspoons RED CURRY PASTE (page 188)

20 ml/¾ fl oz fish sauce

200 ml/6½ fl oz coconut milk

2 ripe tomatoes, quartered

vegetable oil, for deep-frying

1 large eggplant/aubergine (about 400 g/13 oz), diced
  or cut into strips

2 large red Chinese *or* Dutch chillies, split lengthwise
  and seeded

1 × 1.5–1.8 kg/3–4 lb Chinese roasted duck, cut into bite-
  size chunks (discard bones)

4 kaffir lime leaves, finely shredded

steamed rice, to serve

½ cup Thai/holy basil leaves

1 Heat coconut cream in a pot and, when boiling, add RED CURRY PASTE and fish sauce. Simmer gently, uncovered, for 10 minutes. **2** Add coconut milk and tomato and simmer for another 10 minutes. **3** Heat oil to 180°C/350°F in a deep-fryer or large pot and fry eggplant in batches for 4 minutes, or until golden. Drain on paper towel. **4** Deep-fry chilli halves for 1 minute, or until slightly coloured. Drain on paper towel. **5** Add roasted duck chunks to curry, stir and cook gently until duck is heated through. Add lime leaves, fried eggplant and chilli. Stir to combine. **6** Remove from heat and serve with steamed rice, garnished with basil leaves.

Serves 4

Combination fried rice

vegetable oil

1 small onion, diced

2 cloves garlic, finely chopped

4 teaspoons RED CURRY PASTE (page 188)

2 teaspoons caster sugar

200 g/6½ oz cooked prawns/shrimp, shelled

100 g/3½ oz cooked chicken, shredded

100 g/3½ oz cha siew/Chinese red roasted pork slices

3 eggs, beaten

800 g/1 lb 10 oz cooked jasmine (long-grain) rice

40 ml/1¼ fl oz fish sauce

1 red capsicum/bell pepper, finely chopped

40 g/1¼ oz green beans, sliced into fine rounds

4 green onions/scallions, finely sliced

½ cup Thai/holy basil leaves

¼ cup coriander/cilantro/Chinese parsley leaves

2 tablespoons Fried Shallot Slices (page 201)

1 Heat a little oil in a large wok and fry onion and garlic until starting to colour. Add RED CURRY PASTE and sugar and stir to combine. 2 Add prawns, chicken and pork and toss over heat to combine. Transfer from wok to a large plate. 3 Heat a little more oil in the wok and add eggs. Cook until they begin to scramble. As they begin to set, stir in rice and fry for about 2 minutes, or until heated through. Add fish sauce, capsicum and beans. 4 Return prawn mixture to wok and toss to combine thoroughly. Stir in green onion, basil and coriander and remove from heat. 5 Arrange fried rice on a serving plate and sprinkle with fried shallot slices.

Serves 4

Note: Vary this recipe by using lobster meat or yabbies instead of prawns. Or substitute cooked, thinly sliced beef or lamb fillet or ham for the chicken and pork. Fried slices of Chinese/lap cheong or Thai pork sausage are also a delicious addition.

400 ml/12½ fl oz coconut milk

80 ml/2½ fl oz Tamarind Liquid (page 200)

8 teaspoons RED CURRY PASTE (page 188)

400 g/13 oz beef topside, cut into 2.5 cm/1 in cubes

1 stalk lemongrass, cut into 5 cm/2 in lengths

2 kaffir lime leaves

1 litre/32 fl oz Beef/Veal Stock (page 203)

20 ml/¾ fl oz fish sauce

1 tablespoon sugar

200 g/6½ oz fresh bamboo shoots, sliced lengthwise

2 large red Chinese *or* Dutch chillies, sliced

¼ cup Thai/holy basil leaves

Red curry beef soup

1 Bring coconut milk, tamarind liquid and RED CURRY PASTE to boiling point in a pot. Simmer uncovered, stirring constantly, for 5 minutes. **2** Add beef, lemongrass and lime leaves. Reduce heat to a low simmer and cook gently for 40 minutes. **3** Add stock, fish sauce and sugar and return to simmering point. Continue to simmer for another 30 minutes, or until beef is very tender. Taste and, if necessary, adjust seasoning. **4** Add bamboo shoots and chilli and cook for 15 minutes. **5** Ladle soup into bowls, top with basil and serve.

Serves 4

Basics

The following preparations are used at various times throughout this book – most of them are standbys with which good cooks need to be familiar. Making and freezing stock when you can, preparing sauces from summer produce for winter use, keeping sugar syrup and tamarind liquid at the ready mean that your culinary repertoire can expand as if by magic. If you put the effort in when you have the time, you can reap the benefits when you don't – and enjoy the fruits of your labours.

CHINESE FIVE-SPICE POWDER

5 star anise
4 teaspoons fennel seeds
4 teaspoons Sichuan peppercorns
2 teaspoons cloves
1 teaspoon ground cassia
1 teaspoon freshly ground cinnamon

Grind spices to a fine powder, then pass through a fine mesh sieve and discard husks. Store in a sealed jar.
Makes about 4 tablespoons

Note: Ready-prepared Chinese five-spice powder is also available commercially.

SICHUAN SPICE SALT

2 tablespoons sea salt
2 teaspoons Sichuan peppercorns
1 teaspoon Chinese five-spice powder (see above)

Dry-roast sea salt and peppercorns over gentle heat until fragrant and lightly coloured. Cool. Grind to a fine powder, then pass through a fine mesh sieve and discard husks. Mix with five-spice powder and store in a sealed jar.
Makes about 3 tablespoons

Note: Ready-prepared Sichuan spice salt is also available commercially.

GARAM MASALA

seeds from 16 green cardamom pods
1 teaspoon nigella seeds
1 teaspoon cloves
2 teaspoons black peppercorns
¼ teaspoon freshly grated nutmeg
¼ teaspoon ground cassia

Grind whole spices to a fine powder, then stir in remaining spices. Store in a sealed jar.
Makes about 2 tablespoons

Note: Ready-prepared garam masala is also available commercially.

SWEET CHILLI SAUCE

200 ml/6½ fl oz Sugar Syrup (page 201)
160 ml/5 fl oz strained lime juice
80 ml/2½ fl oz fish sauce
2 teaspoons chopped red birds-eye chilli
2 teaspoons minced garlic

Combine ingredients and refrigerate until ready to use. Keeps, refrigerated, for up to 1 week.
Makes about 400 ml/13 fl oz

Note: Ready-prepared sweet chilli sauce is also available commercially.

TAMARIND LIQUID

The most refined way to use tamarind is to make tamarind liquid, getting maximum flavour without the coarse, fibrous texture of the pulp. Simmer 1 part tamarind pulp to 4 parts water for 30 minutes or so, then pass pulp and water through a coarse mesh or conical sieve. Discard fibre and seeds. Tamarind liquid keeps, refrigerated, for up to 1 month.

SAFFRON BUTTER

Stir into sauces at the last minute to enrich flavour.

50 ml/1½ fl oz Tomato Essence (see below)
½ teaspoon saffron threads
250 g/8 oz unsalted butter, softened

Bring tomato essence to the boil in a small saucepan, add saffron and infuse for a few minutes only. Whip butter in a food processor and gradually blend in saffron liquid until incorporated. Keeps, refrigerated in a sealed container, for 1 week.
Makes 250 g

TOMATO ESSENCE

An exquisite way of adding the intense flavour of summer's best tomatoes to sauces and the like, and a great way of extending the season, via freezing. Pulp tomatoes and drain in a jelly bag or double layer of

muslin suspended over a bowl for 24 hours. To keep essence clear, do not push or force pulp through bag. To make reduced tomato essence, bring essence to the boil and reduce by half. This increases the sweetness slightly and intensifies the flavour. Freeze in ice-cube trays for later use. (Use the remaining pulp as tomato purée.)
2.5 kg/5 lb tomatoes yield about 500 ml/16 fl oz essence

SUGAR SYRUP

Bring an equal quantity of caster sugar and water to the boil and cook for about 5 minutes, or until sugar has dissolved. Cool. Sugar syrup keeps indefinitely and can also be made with brown sugar. If preferred, you can substitute 4 teaspoons caster sugar for each 30 ml/1 fl oz sugar syrup called for in a recipe.
1 cup water and 1 cup sugar yield about 1½ cups sugar syrup

TEMPURA BATTER

¾ cup plain/all-purpose flour
1 egg, lightly beaten
200 ml iced soda water
½ teaspoon sea salt
¼ teaspoon freshly ground black pepper

Work flour into egg in a bowl. Add soda water and mix roughly with a chopstick. Season with salt and pepper. The batter should be slightly lumpy, not smooth. Refrigerate until ready to use. Add extra soda water if batter looks too thick.

CARAMELISED ONION

Serve as a condiment, use as a tart filling or even add to bread dough. Cook finely sliced sweet brown onions in a good quantity of olive oil in a wide, heavy-based pan over moderate heat until onion caramelises and tastes sweet. Strain, reserving the flavoured oil for other cooking. Keeps, refrigerated in a sealed container, for up to 2 weeks.

WHOLE ROASTED SHALLOTS

Roast shallots in a little olive oil in a wide, heavy-based pan over moderate heat until soft and sweet. Strain, reserving the flavoured oil for other cooking. Keeps, refrigerated, for up to 2 weeks.

FRIED SHALLOT SLICES

Made from red Asian shallots, these crisp, wafery slices can be sprinkled over stir-fries, noodle dishes, curries and so on for a richly flavoured texture contrast. They can be bought from Asian food stores, but are easy to make at home. Slice red shallots finely lengthwise and fry in a good quantity of vegetable oil over moderate heat until golden brown – the shallots should float freely in the oil as they cook. Remove pan from heat immediately and pour the hot oil through a sieve into a stainless steel bowl. Spread fried shallots on paper towel to drain and cool. Reserve flavoured oil for other cooking. Store shallots in a sealed container to keep them crisp.

FRIED GARLIC SLICES

Garlic cloves can be sliced finely and cooked and stored in the same manner as Fried Shallot Slices (see above).

FISH STOCK

heads and bones of 2 large fish
6 green onions/scallions, chopped
1 knob ginger, sliced
1 teaspoon white peppercorns
500 ml/16 fl oz dry white wine
cold water

Wash fish heads thoroughly to remove all blood. Discard gills as they will make the stock bitter. Put all ingredients into a stockpot, adding cold water to cover. Bring to the boil and simmer on low heat, skimming frequently to remove any scum, for 2 hours. Strain through a conical sieve, pressing to extract as much juice as possible. Discard solids. Strain again through a fine mesh sieve

to remove all sediment. Cool and refrigerate or freeze, unless using immediately.
Makes about 3 litres/96 fl oz

Note: Use good-quality, fresh, cleaned fish heads and bones as they will affect the flavour of the stock. Any deep-sea white-fleshed fish is suitable.

PRAWN/SHRIMP STOCK

6 medium-size tomatoes
1 kg/2 lb prawn/shrimp heads and shells
100 ml/3½ fl oz Chinese Shaoxing rice wine
50 ml/1½ fl oz vegetable oil
1 medium-size brown onion, chopped
6 cloves garlic, sliced
3 slices ginger
2 slices galangal
1 stalk lemongrass, finely sliced
2 red birds-eye chillies, chopped
1 teaspoon Sichuan peppercorns
1 teaspoon fennel seeds
1 star anise
2 kaffir lime leaves, chopped
3 litres/96 fl oz Fish Stock (page 201)

Preheat oven to moderately hot (200°C/400°F) and roast whole tomatoes for 20 minutes, or until coloured and softened. Heat a large wok and add prawn heads and shells. Toss over high heat until they start to colour, then add rice wine and stir, scraping to dissolve all browned bits in pan. Remove from heat. Heat oil in a stockpot and add remaining ingredients, except stock. Cook over moderate heat until mixture starts to colour and become aromatic. Add cooked prawn heads and shells and their juices, tomatoes and stock. Bring to the boil and simmer for 2 hours, skimming frequently to remove any scum. Strain through a conical sieve, pressing to extract as much juice as possible. Discard solids. Strain again through a fine mesh sieve to remove all sediment. Cool and refrigerate or freeze, unless using immediately.
Makes about 3 litres/96 fl oz

Note: Lobster or crab stock can be made in the same manner.

WHITE CHICKEN STOCK

1 chicken carcass
1 free-range, corn-fed chicken
several slices ginger
handful of green onion/scallion tops
several white peppercorns, freshly cracked
500 ml/16 fl oz dry white wine
cold water

Wash chicken carcass in cold water to remove all blood. Put all ingredients into a stockpot and add cold water to cover. Bring to the boil over low heat and simmer, skimming frequently to remove any scum, for 2 hours. Remove solids carefully (strip meat from chicken and keep for another use) and discard bones. Strain stock through a fine mesh sieve to remove all sediment. Cool and refrigerate or freeze, unless using immediately.
Makes about 3 litres/96 fl oz

BROWN CHICKEN STOCK

Roasting the bones and vegetables makes this stock darker and more flavoursome than its more subtle white counterpart.

1.5 kg/3 lb chicken carcasses
125 ml/4 fl oz red wine
6 medium-size tomatoes
vegetable oil
1 medium-size brown onion, chopped
2 medium-size carrots, chopped
1 bulb/head garlic, cut in half
3 green onions/scallions, chopped
1 knob ginger, sliced
1 bay leaf
½ teaspoon black peppercorns
handful of flat-leaf parsley
2.5 litres/80 fl oz White Chicken Stock (see above)

Preheat oven to moderately hot (200°C/400°F). Brown chicken carcasses in a roasting tray to render some of their fat. Add wine and deglaze pan to dissolve all browned bits. While bones are browning, roast whole tomatoes in another pan for 20 minutes, or until coloured and softened. Heat a little oil in a large stockpot and

cook onion, carrot, garlic, green onion and ginger until fragrant. Stir in bay leaf, peppercorns and parsley, then add browned bones and pan juices, tomatoes and stock. Bring to the boil and simmer, uncovered, for 3–4 hours, skimming frequently to remove fat and scum. Strain stock through a conical sieve, pressing firmly to extract as much juice as possible. Discard solids. Strain again through a fine mesh sieve to remove all sediment. Allow to settle and remove any fat that rises to the top. Return stock to rinsed-out pot, bring to the boil and reduce slightly for a thicker consistency and richer flavour, if required. Cool and refrigerate or freeze, unless using immediately.
Makes about 3 litres/96 fl oz

Note: Make duck stock in a similar manner when you have used the meat for another purpose – the bones have far too much flavour to throw out after only one use.

RED BRAISING STOCK

A master stock for red braising is a mandatory preparation in the kitchens of northern China. This stock should never be thrown out – as long as it is brought to the boil every week, and is kept refrigerated in a sealed container, it will grow better and richer with age and can be kept topped up. Every time you cook meat in it, just make sure you strain the stock through a fine mesh sieve before refrigerating (this keeps it free of particles that may cause bacteria to grow). My master stock is now eight years old and I use it constantly as I am addicted to food cooked in it.

This master stock gives a rich, reddish-brown, lacquered appearance and a wonderfully penetrating flavour and aroma to meat and poultry. As Ken Hom says in the *Encyclopedia of Chinese Cookery Techniques*, it is a stock 'that is at once salty from the two types of soy sauces; sweet from the sugar; spicy on account of the peppercorns, anise and fennel seeds; and mellow from the rice wine'. As the process of red braising is a very gentle one, it also gives anything cooked in it a tender, velvety texture.

3 litres/96 fl oz White Chicken Stock (page 202)
300 ml/10 fl oz dark soy sauce

250 ml/8 fl oz soy sauce
100 ml/3½ fl oz Chinese Shaoxing rice wine
40 g/1¼ oz Chinese yellow rock sugar (available from Asian/Chinese food stores)
2 star anise, broken
2 pieces cassia bark
1 teaspoon fennel seeds
1 teaspoon Sichuan peppercorns
1 black cardamom pod, cracked
2 pieces dried orange peel
2 red birds-eye chillies, split lengthwise
4 slices ginger
2 slices fresh galangal
3 pieces liquorice root

Bring all ingredients to the boil in a large stockpot. Simmer on very low heat for 1 hour, then strain through a fine mesh sieve. Discard solids. Cool completely before refrigerating in a sealed container.
Makes about 4 litres/128 fl oz

BEEF/VEAL STOCK

This is a rich stock, made from roasted beef bones, shanks and veal knuckles, that forms the basis of good sauces and soups with great depth of flavour.

1 kg/2 lb beef bones
1 kg/2 lb split shanks
1 kg/2 lb veal knuckles
5 medium-size tomatoes, halved
2 medium-size brown onions, chopped
1 large carrot, chopped
vegetable oil
500 ml/16 fl oz red wine
handful of flat-leaf parsley
4 teaspoons black peppercorns
2 sprigs of thyme
cold water

Preheat oven to moderately hot (200°C/400°F) and brown bones in a roasting tray for 30 minutes. While bones are cooking, toss whole tomatoes with onion, carrot and a little oil in another roasting tray and roast until softened. Put bones into a large stockpot – there should be room to spare. Remove any fat from baking

dish, add wine and deglaze pan to dissolve all browned bits. Tip wine and juices into stock. Add vegetables to stockpot with remaining ingredients and cover with cold water. Bring to the boil, reduce heat and simmer for 6 hours, skimming regularly to remove scum. Carefully remove bones and strain stock through a conical sieve. Discard solids. Strain again through a fine mesh sieve to remove all sediment. Skim off any excess fat from surface with a ladle. Cool and refrigerate or freeze, unless using immediately. If your recipe calls for reduced stock or a demi-glace, simply cook stock until its volume is reduced and it becomes thicker and more unctuous – demi-glace should coat the back of a spoon.
Makes about 5 litres/160 fl oz

SPICED VEGETABLE STOCK

This versatile vegetable stock can be made ahead of time. It can be used as a base for a vegetable curry, added to a stir-fry or enriched with coconut milk to make a sauce.

1 bulb/head garlic
6 dried Chinese black mushrooms
500 ml/16 fl oz warm water
30 ml/1 fl oz vegetable oil
1 medium-size brown onion, chopped
2 carrots, peeled and finely sliced
1 stalk celery (with leaves), chopped
1 tablespoon minced ginger
5 green onions/scallions, sliced
3 red birds-eye chillies, sliced
2 teaspoons black peppercorns
2 teaspoons Sichuan peppercorns
1 tablespoon minced fresh turmeric
2 litres/64 fl oz cold water
1 stalk lemongrass, finely sliced
50 ml/1½ fl oz fish sauce

Preheat oven to moderate (180°C/350°F). Wrap garlic in aluminium foil and roast for 30 minutes, or until softened. Unwrap and separate the cloves. Meanwhile, soak dried mushrooms in warm water for 15 minutes, or until softened. Heat oil in a stockpot and sweat onion, carrot, celery, ginger, green onion, chilli and roasted garlic over low heat for about 15 minutes, or until softened. Add

mushrooms and their soaking liquid, black and Sichuan peppercorns, turmeric and cold water and bring to the boil. Simmer for 30 minutes. Add lemongrass and fish sauce and simmer for a further 15 minutes. Strain through a fine mesh sieve. Discard solids. Cool and refrigerate or freeze, unless using immediately.
Makes about 2 litres/64 fl oz

EGG NOODLES

The following quantities are sufficient for the dishes in this book that include egg noodles. However, if you want to make noodles the feature of a meal, just increase the quantities – simply multiply the ingredients as required.

3 large eggs
20 ml/¾ fl oz olive oil
250 g/8 oz bread flour
pinch of sea salt
rice flour, for dusting

Blend all ingredients, except rice flour, in a food processor until dough forms a ball. Wrap in plastic film and refrigerate for 1 hour. Cut dough into 4 pieces and flatten each piece by hand or with a rolling pin. Pass each piece through rollers of a pasta machine, starting on the widest setting and working your way through each setting until you reach the finest. Dust dough with rice flour each time before moving onto next setting to prevent sticking (rice flour is free of glutens, which could toughen the dough at this stage). Hang sheets of dough over a broom handle or back of a chair to dry for 10 minutes – this makes dough easier to cut. Pass through spaghetti cutters on your pasta machine, then hang noodles over a broom handle or back of a chair for 30 minutes, or until ready to cook. Bring a large saucepan of water to a rolling boil, add noodles and allow water to return to the boil. Cook for 2 minutes, remove noodles with a sieve and drain. If not eating immediately, refresh noodles under cold running water to stop them cooking, then drain and toss lightly with a little oil to prevent sticking. To reheat, immerse noodles in boiling water for 10 seconds, then drain.
Serves 3–4 as a main course

INDEX